FORD GT40

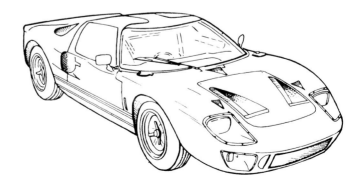

FORD GT40

An Anglo-American supercar classic

DAVID HODGES

MRP

MRP PUBLISHING LTD
PO Box 1318, Croydon CR9 5YP, England

First Edition published 1984
Second Edition published 1998
Reprinted 2003

British Library Cataloguing in Publication Data:
A catalogue record for this book is available from the British Library

ISBN 1-899870-25-3

Printed in Great Britain by
The Amadeus Press, Cleckheaton, West Yorkshire

Bound by MPG Books Ltd, Bodmin, Cornwall

Contents

Introduction

It is almost impossible to overstate Ford's impact on motorsport in the 1960s, from single-seater racing to rallies, but above all in endurance racing with the GT40. On the other hand, it is sometimes easy to overlook this car as a true forerunner of the supercars produced through the last three decades. In the GT40, Ford built a car that now seems timeless, a car that has a prosaic iron-block engine yet shatteringly defeated much-lauded thoroughbreds on circuits, and showed exotic constructors the lines to follow in the layout of high-performance road cars.

Ford set out to win a classic motor race with the GT40, and that was seen as an end in itself. In the mid-1960s, thoughts that the company might be setting trends cannot have entered corporate minds, nor can thoughts that a quarter of a century later the car would be one of the most evocative in the thriving historic car environment and that GT40s would still be reaping image – publicity – bonuses for Ford.

The story is complex, and can seem muddled. In America, the car was often referred to as the Ford GT in the 1960s. Some company men still lump the four distinct types together as 'GT40' – maybe the general image is more important than veracity – so it is worth recalling that the GT40 was the original car, the Mk II was wholly recognizable as a second version, and the Mk III as an obvious attempt to build a refined road car third version (there were no contemporary Ford references to a 'GT40 Mk II', although some company literature did refer to the 'GT40 Mk III').

While the Mk IV followed on in the same sportscar programme, it was a very different machine. Apart from the general layout, the engine and the transmission, it had little in common with the GT40. The GT40s, the Mk II and the Mk III were Anglo-American cars; the Mk IV was all-American, and the first American car to win the Le Mans 24-hour race. In a fascinating twist, it did so after the Mk II version of the GT40 had won the French classic, but before a GT40 scored an historic double victory at Le Mans . . .

That victory, in the race for which the GT40 was conceived, did not come until Ford had turned away from the car, and incidentally when it had been raced in the front line for five years. The victorious car was run by the independent JWA-Gulf team, which had carried on GT40 development to 'works' standards. Beyond that, most of the cars produced for sale were intended for circuit use, perhaps less ambitiously. They proved to be ideal private entrants' machines – sturdy, reliable and quick. That was so in the 1960s, and it holds good in modern historic events.

The GT40 was functional and handsome, and a model of compact packaging of mechanical elements and accommodation. It was never easy to get into – those run-and-jump Le Mans starts must have been challenging – but the cockpit was comfortable and did not enforce a difficult splayed-legs driving position or present an awkwardly-angled steering wheel. At anything but low speeds it was a light car to drive, and save for grip (by modern standards) or problems stemming from weight distribution that familiarity could overcome, it had few vices. It was civilized, and in its weight there was the reassurance of strength. The promise of lots of performance was ever-present.

Original build quality was a great shortcoming, and at least that has been overcome in cossetted survivors (most of the cars built are still in use). If there is virtue in replicas, it is in the best, like Safir's Mk V, which show what Ford could have done with its supercar in the 1960s, and should have done with it if there had been the will to continue with a very small, ultra-specialist, operation . . .

These Fords, and the men associated with them, are the essence of an exciting and significant chapter in motoring and motor racing history, which this book attempts to recall in perspective.

Acknowledgements

This is a new edition, and in writing the original I was helped by the late Len Bailey, Michael Bowler, Harry Calton. Bryan Wingfield, and the late John Wyer and David Yorke, and this book still benefits from their assistance.

Ronnie Spain's painstaking archive has been valuable, and I am also grateful to John Allen, Ray Christopher, Gordon Bruce and Peter Loweth, James M Glickenhaus, Adrian Hamilton, Gordon Jones, Rod Leach, Jim Rose, Peter Thorp and GT40 owners. John Blunsden has twice been an understanding publisher.

The illustrations come from many sources: John Allen, Ken Attwell, Alice Bixler, Al Bochroch, the Ford Motor Company, Geoff Goddard, GTD, the Gulf Oil Corporation, Ray Hutton, Pat Murphy, Jim Rose, Maurice Rowe, William Stone and Peter Thorp, as well as the archives of *Autocar* and the sadly missed *Motor*, and a personal collection.

David Hodges

1

Total Performance

The Anglo-American concept

In the 1960s, the Ford Motor Company became a powerful force in international motor racing – a fact which can be recalled simply enough today, but when that decade opened, such a state of affairs would have been almost beyond imagination . . .

In the USA, Ford had been a party to the Automobile Manufacturers Association 1957 agreement not to participate in racing, or indeed in any public speed contest, to the extent of not even supplying official cars, for example pace cars. It hurt. General Motors had launched a new Chevrolet V8 range with an exciting image just before the 'ban' was agreed, while Fords of the period were generally stolid. There was the Thunderbird, but that had never become the sportscar American enthusiasts had hoped it would in the mid-1950s – Ford had never pretended it was a sportscar – and by 1958 it had put on weight and bulk to become another mundane sedan. In contrast, Chevrolet's Corvette was still distinctly sporty.

The AMA agreement was at odds with the times, in any case. More than ever before the car-buying public was youthful, ripe to respond to an image of high performance and excitement. Manufacturers were tending to disregard the spirit of the agreement, and – over-simplifying the creeping build-up to an almost inevitable decision – Henry Ford II tore up the agreement in the summer of 1962. (More pompously, Ford 'notified the board of directors of the Automobile Manufacturers Association that we feel we can better establish our own standards of conduct with respect to the manner in which the performance of our vehicles is to be promoted'.)

The American Ford Division was committed to racing again, and a 'Total Performance' image was to be cultivated. Initially, the racing effort was directed to the American market, to stock and drag racing, and international attention was attracted by Ford's Indianapolis programme with Lotus, the improbable but so-nearly successful Falcons run in the 1963 Monte Carlo rally, and even the detail of private Galaxies suddenly upsetting the well-established pattern of British saloon car racing.

That year, Ford decided to challenge the Europeans in a genuinely international racing field. Logically – at that time – the choice fell on endurance racing, where one European race meant at least something to ordinary Americans, where American entrants had come close to major European success in the past, and where the cars could be shown to bear some relationship to the company's normal products, or at least to its new image. The one event that meant so much was, of course, the Le Mans 24-hour race, the classic *Grand Prix d'Endurance*, which unfailingly (but sometimes quite disproportionately) fascinated the general public of the Western world.

Much was made of the benefits to be derived from endurance races run largely 'on normal highways', in a well-publicized rub-off on mainline products, with references to 'GT sports vehicles' being 'closely allied to normal passenger vehicles which encountered all the problems of highway driving including handling, driver environment, braking, stability and safety'.

Endurance racing championships through much of the 1950s and into the 1960s were dominated by Ferrari: in the nine seasons of the original World Sports Car Championship, Ferrari won seven times, beaten by Mercedes-Benz in 1955 and Aston Martin in 1959, and when parallel GT and Prototype Championships were introduced Ferrari won both in 1962-63. The Ferrari record at Le Mans was erratic until the 1960s opened, with victories in 1949, 1954 and 1958, then the 1960 race saw the first of a series of victories for the Italian marque.

The 1963 race was to be closely analyzed by Ford to provide a target: 200mph capability, with a lap speed of 130mph and a 24-hour average of 120mph. The basic configuration of a car – mid-engined – was in effect predetermined for Ford, although it was alien to American traditions. The trend towards mid-engined sportscars was firmly established by 1963, when Le Mans fell to a mid-engined car

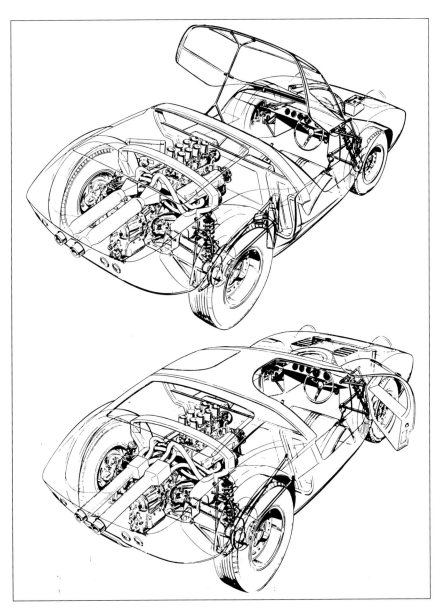

The GT40 was first visualized as a car with side radiators like the Mustang I and a front-hinged cockpit canopy. The lower drawing is much closer to the final product, with radiators moved into the nose and a fixed roof into which the doors were deeply recessed.

for the first time (a 3-litre V12 Ferrari 250P).

Enzo Ferrari had felt his way cautiously into this new era, the pressure in racing coming from the success of mid-engined Coopers in the Grands Prix of the late 1950s rather than from the then-distant threat of rear-engined sports-racing Porsches. In 1959-60 Cooper and Lotus had introduced sports-racing cars, the Monaco and 19 (sometimes referred to as the Monte Carlo) respectively, closely based on their Grand Prix cars. Ferrari had been forced to follow the British constructors' leads, with the V6-engined Dino 246 Formula 1 car in 1960 and the 246SP sports-racing car in 1961. Despite a considerable upheaval when chief engineer Carlo Chiti, team manager Romolo Tavoni and others had left at the end of 1961, the team had come to terms with mid-engined cars. It had reverted to V12 engines in the shapely 250P run in endurance events; this was to be succeeded by the 3.3-litre 275P/275LM and the 4-litre 330P, and those were the cars for Ford to shoot at.

To the end of 'Total Performance', short cuts were quite acceptable, and an Indianapolis programme with Lotus was already under way early in 1963 when the possibility of a liaison that would give direct access to European sports-racing expertise arose. Ford negotiated to buy Ferrari.

Word that Ferrari might be for sale was passed to Ford in Germany in 1960, but seemingly this was not followed up and Ford made an approach through its Italian company two years later. Negotiations took place in 1963, when Ferrari's price was apparently $18 million – just a few million pounds – and hardly a substantial amount in Ford terms (the Edsel flop of the late 1950s had reputedly cost the company more than ten times that amount).

A Ford team thoroughly investigated every aspect of the Maranello factory – in hindsight it seems remarkable that they should have been permitted access to make a complete inventory, and it indicates how serious Ferrari was. The basis of a deal that came tantalizingly close to fulfilment was a projected pair of companies, Ford-Ferrari and Ferrari-Ford.

Ford was to have a 90 per cent holding in the first, which would produce high-performance GT cars and give Ford a prestige road car line to boost its new image. Ferrari was to retain a 90 per cent holding in Ferrari-Ford, which would build and race competition cars.

In mid-May 1953, a positive conclusion to these negotiations seemed to be in sight, but Enzo Ferrari began to realize that he would lose the autonomy he thought he would retain in Ferrari-Ford, and he started to back-pedal. Negotiations broke down, although there were hints that they could have been re-opened more than once before Fiat eventually stepped in, showing much more respect for Enzo Ferrari and probably more tact in their dealings.

It has been forcefully argued that the popular impression misleads, and that Ford

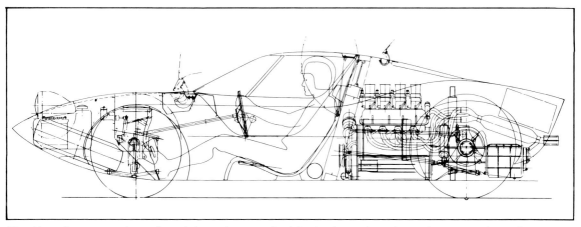

The side-radiator proposal was discarded once it was realized that intakes at the optimum size to serve the cooling purpose would ruin the clean lines, and this elevation drawing shows a development close to the final GT40 layout. Retractable lights were to be abandoned as the nose height was reduced because of worries about lift – this shape suggests a car that wants to become airborne! Packaging is tight, and in an oddity the pedals are not floor-mounted.

A clay model of the original design study. Had this shape been adopted, the smooth nose lines would have been broken by the pop-up headlamps.

did not set out to beat Ferrari – beating the world at Le Mans was what mattered. But in the early 1960s that meant beating Ferrari, for there were no other cars of consequence in contention for an outright win: there were Maseratis, which seldom lasted long, there were Aston Martins that – with the possible exception of the 212 and 215 in 1962-63 – were hardly new, there were lightweight E-type Jaguars that performed creditably but were hardly competition for Ferrari's out-and-out sports-racers, and there were a Lister and a Lola GT in 1963. Ferrari won the 1960-63 races, with as many as 15 cars officially or privately entered in 1962, and 11 or 12 in the other years. So to beat the world in this arena, Ford had to beat Ferrari . . .

Throughout the negotiations, Ford had fall-back positions, being prepared to go it alone or seek another liaison (by inference with a British constructor, as elsewhere there were then few of any consequence). A Special Vehicles Department was formally established, around the nucleus of a research and styling group headed by Yorkshire-born Royston (Roy) Lunn, once Jowett's chief engineer and then a development engineer with Ford of Britain until he took on an executive role with the parent company in America in 1958.

This group had been responsible for Mustang I, a 1.7-litre mid-engined open two-seater which had been shown to the public in 1962, to test reactions (the number was applied retrospectively as the production Mustang was introduced).

This little sportscar was an element in Ford's approach to an essential revision of its image, and it was as important for the part it played in convincing company men as in demonstrating changing attitudes to the public. It was built quickly, using a Ford (Germany) Taunus 1.5-litre V4 and some Ford (of Britain) Cortina components, with a spaceframe and attractive aluminium bodywork riding on distinctive Lotus wheels. The engine was behind the cockpit, wind-tunnel work led to radiator air intakes in low-pressure areas, Ford's infant computer department was employed in suspension design, and there were details such as a fixed driver's seat with adjustable pedals and steering column. Altogether, it was a convincing exercise, and it brought together an enthusiastic group.

As far as the Mustang programme was concerned it was a feint, and while it was to be easy to point to similarities, later assertions that it was the progenitor of the GT40 were, let us say, good public relations material. More to the point, a group of Ford executives, including Lunn, headed for England to set up a collaboration in the highly-specialized field of racing car design and construction. Effectively there were two possibilities, Lotus and Lola, for although the Coopers' intuitive engineering had earlier changed fundamental approaches to the layout of competition cars, it was felt that their operation was unsophisticated in the 1960s. Aston Martin was also considered (and Ford was soundly rebuffed by David Brown). Concern that the GT might become another Lotus-Ford – as the Indianapolis cars quite justifiably were – led to Eric Broadley.

Coincidentally, Broadley had a complete Lola that was almost a prototype for the car taking shape in Ford minds, a low, sleek GT coupe first displayed at the London Racing Car Show in January 1963. Its central structure was a monocoque, with tubular frames front and rear. It was then rare among European competition cars in that its power unit was American, a pushrod overhead-valve 4,262cc (260cu in) Ford V8. This was mounted ahead of the rear axle line, and drove through a Colotti four-speed gearbox in unit with the final drive (transaxle).

The Ford team, headed by Donald Frey, and including Ray Geddes as well as Lunn, started talking to Broadley almost as soon as the Ferrari negotiations broke down. By that time, the Lola GT had made its racing debut, showing no more than promise in its first two international races, the Nürburgring 1,000kms and Le Mans. The outcome was that Ford to all intents and purposes took over Lola for a period and Broadley was co-opted to work with Lunn to develop the design of the Ford

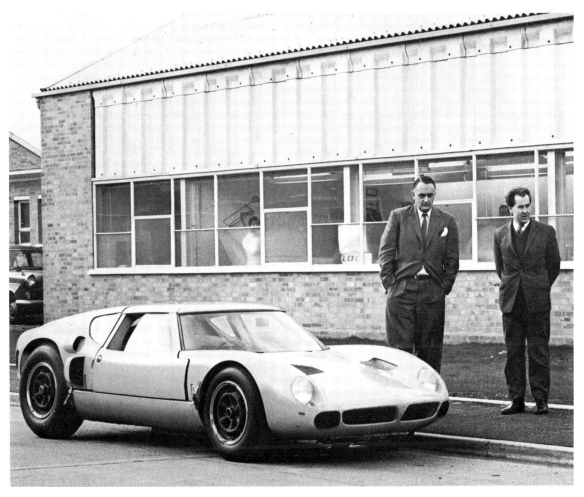

Progenitor of the GT40. A Lola GT parked outside the Lola Cars drawing office at Slough, with John Wyer and Eric Broadley appearing less than enthusiastic about a photo call

GT, under a two-year contract to run from August 1963.

It had already been decided that the cars would be built in England, although the Lola 'factory' was far from being a suitable base. (This humble establishment in a Bromley side street was a typical racing car boutique of the time – cramped, cold in winter and hot in summer, with a small general office up rickety stairs, certainly nothing so pretentious as a drawing office, and shop floor space for only a handful of cars.) Matters like accommodation fell into the province of another recruit to the management team, one-time Aston Martin racing manager John Wyer, who became the European manager of what was then Ford's Special Vehicles Activity. In time he was to set up Ford Advanced Vehicles as a subsidiary of Ford of Britain, but meanwhile he was to establish a base for the GT operation at Slough (and come to terms with the American way of doing things). Three design engineers, Len Bailey, Ron Martin and Chuck Mountain, became temporary residents at the Lola premises in Bromley until, in the autumn of 1963, the Slough plant was ready.

The project had been moving ahead, for the target dates for the car's debut – and in the minds of some US Ford executives its instant success – were very tight. Concept studies in the USA had merged into design studies and crystalized in a full-size clay model and a ⅜-scale near-replica for wind-tunnel tests. The clay had sleek lines, which in many aspects

were to be echoed by the GT40. These early designs envisaged a mid-engined coupe, with some outward features later to be dropped – a forward-hinged canopy (there was concern that this might be ruled out by the regulations), twin radiators located behind the cockpit with side ducting (analysis suggested that these would be inadequate) and retractable headlights (it was feared that these might be impractical).

At this stage, the engine was to be the 4.2-litre (256cu in) V8 developed for the Indianapolis programme, and a Colotti transaxle was to be used. The overall 'package' envisaged a vehicle with a wheelbase of 95in (241cm), overall length of 156in (396cm) and that overall height of 40in (102cm) which was to lead to the designation 'GT40'. These parameters were to be met in the actual car – the track to the inch and the height within half an inch, although the overall length was eventually 165in (419cm). By coincidence, the Ferrari 250P had an identical wheelbase, and closely similar track dimensions.

Towards the end of 1963, one of the two Lola GTs available (the first and third cars – the other had been delivered to John Mecom) was used in a component test programme run at British circuits and at Monza, when the drivers were Bruce McLaren and Roy Salvadori. Some of the objectives were achieved, for example in checking suspension and driveline components and the cooling system intended for the GT40. Fast times were

Mustang I was a persuasive concept car, and a realistic one as it was very much a runner. It played a part in the GT40 programme as a lead-in – convincing Ford management and bringing together a team of like-minded designers and engineers.

not an objective, although unofficially the Lola was lapped within a second of the Monza GT record, and curiously, no duration runs were attempted to extend the transmission (in particular) of a car intended for endurance racing. The road behaviour of the Lola was found to have shortcomings at high speeds, and misleading interpretations led to this flaw being carried through to the early GT40.

There was mounting friction between various members of the team through the winter, while the first cars were being built, and one result was that the programme slipped to the extent that some Dearborn ambitions to see the car make its racing debut at Sebring in March 1964 had to be abandoned. However, a launch in the USA still had top priority. Hard work saw the first car completed on April 1 and, at some cost in precious testing time, this was flown to New York for a press presentation.

The tone of a press release issued to coincide with that event was restrained (the punctuation in this quoted passage is faithful to the original):

Ready to go Racing – at 200 m.p.h.
After less than one year's design and development, the Ford GT is ready to go racing.

The fastest Ford ever built – it reflects the internationalism of the company.

It was designed in the United States, developed and built in Britain, tested in Italy and will make its racing debut in Germany. It is capable of speeds up to 200 m.p.h.

Brothers Under the Skin
Only 40 ins. high and 13 ft. long the Ford GT is of monocoque construction with fibre glass outer panels in the doors, the body ends and the dashboard. It is independently sprung on all four wheels and the Ford 4.2 litre 350 bhp Indianapolis engine is mounted amidships directly behind the driver. The Colotti type 37 four speed gear box and final drive transmits the colossal power of this V8 to the rear wheels while 11½ in. disc brakes are used on all four wheels.

"Our aim" said Roy Lunn, the 39 year old Englishman who is in charge of this exciting new project, "has been to produce a car which will enable us to design, develop and test components and ideas which can be directly applied to our normal passenger car range." And so on – it was a straightforward and factual document.

The Lola GT. In the early 1960s Lola concentrated on single-seaters, but before the Bowmaker support for a Formula 1 programme was withdrawn at the end of 1962, Eric Broadley's thoughts had turned towards the Grand Touring prototype category, and to an extent therefore back towards the sports-racing cars that had made Lola's reputation. In the tradition of show debuts, the first GT was hardly complete when it made its first appearance, and was never to be developed to raceworthiness.

The basis of the central section of the GT was a pair of box-section side sills, which also served as fuel tanks (bags were not used, joints being sealed with a rubber compound). The floorpan and boxed bracing members linked the sills, and tubular subframes ran fore and aft from them. The doors were cut into the roof, and the narrow steel centre section between them contributed little to chassis stiffness. Steel and alloy were used in the construction, even in the sills, where the inner face was in sheet steel and the outer part in duralumin.

Independent suspension all round followed orthodox lines. Bodywork and doors were in glassfibre, and the width of the doors was such that sliding windows could easily be incorporated.

The design envisaged the use of Ford or GM V8s, and the 4,262cc Shelby Cobra Ford unit fitted in the cars raced in 1963 was rated at 260bhp at 6,500rpm, which gave the little Lola a formidable power-to weight ratio of 325bhp/ton.

Principal dimensions: wheelbase, 92in; track, front and rear, 52in; overall length, 154in; overall width, 63in; overall height, 40in.

2

The First GT40

Taking shape

The sleek blue and white coupe flown out of London Airport on April 2, 1964 certainly looked the part. It was not a refined Lola GT – indeed, by comparison with that very straightforward car it could have been considered over-engineered – and it departed considerably from the Ford concept packages, but its clean lines, uncluttered with ornamentation, were convincing. Ford meant business.

The main structure was the monocoque centre-section in 23-gauge sheet steel, folded and pressed, which was considered light enough for any ideas of using light alloy to be set aside at an early stage, on the grounds that it would have no application to production models and, as much to the point, would have required time and resources (although the more experienced British participants in the programme could doubtless have solved problems in this area, given a free hand). The underbody was in unit with the main box side-members, which contained neoprene bag fuel cells holding a total of 37 gallons (168 litres), with an independent filler and electric pump on each side. The bulk of the fuel load was carried forward of the centre of gravity to reduce the rearward weight distribution bias. Front-to-rear balance was 43:57 on the first cars, and not greatly improved on later production versions; considering the weight of the V8, this was commendable, but drivers were to find that it did not pay to let the tail get too far out of line! The two main

bulkheads and the narrow roof 'spine' completed the main part of the chassis, while sheet steel structures fore and aft carried the suspension mountings.

Construction of the chassis was straightforward, Abbey Panels' work being complicated only by some of the fiddly details. It proved to be very rigid, with the sponson side-members contributing great strength (these were a feature of the Lola GT, and the major advance in the Ford was in lateral strength). However, the use of steel was later to make for considerable rust problems for GT40 owners and restorers, while the bag tanks had short lives. They had to live with the horrors of rust. Bag tanks could be replaced properly only with the front suspension and some bodywork removed and much frustrating fiddling (the dubious short cut of hacking into the metal of the sills was to be adopted on some cars). But then, classic car collectors were a long way from Ford minds in the mid-1960s . . .

The body was designed in the USA and a clay master shipped to England, where few changes were made before moulds were taken for the glassfibre panels. Specialized Mouldings was responsible for the first bodies; Glass Fibre Engineering was to undertake the production types. The principal unstressed glassfibre items were the nose and tail panels and the doors, where care was taken to ensure flush fittings (to the same aerodynamic end, window glass was installed with then-new

The partially completed chassis of the first car, *above*, and at a later stage of construction, *below*, with the suspension attached and the 4.2-litre engine installed. The ribbing along the sills was normally clothed by bodywork, although in the later 1960s it was often exposed on circuit cars as the glassfibre covering was removed to save weight. There was no rollcage, but the strength of this construction was later to be proved in accidents where a car rolled, such as Fry's in 1073.

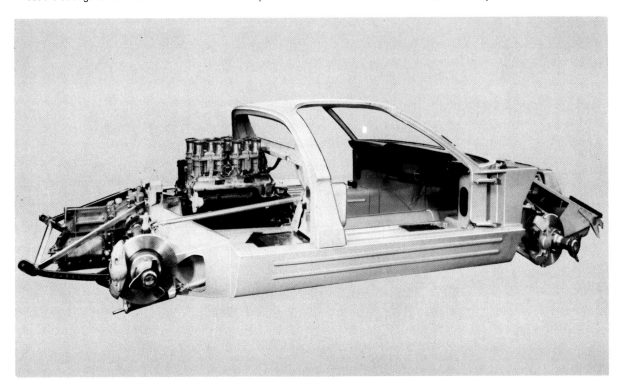

The first car nearing completion at Ford Advanced Vehicles. In the lower picture a Lola GT can be seen in the background, and both photographs give an impression of spacious workshops, which did not seem so generous when production cars were put through.

Front suspension detail. The single-caliper solid brake discs were later to be superseded by ventilated discs.

Despite some gimmicks, like the ventilated seats, the cockpit appeared workmanlike. The handbrake was a rather crude affair; operating it simply depressed the brake pedal. The facia was simple, and the first cars did not have the speedometer that was to be introduced on the left. A large rev-counter was positioned to be read through the upper half of the steering wheel; lesser gauges were for amps, water and oil pressure, and oil temperature on the right.

19

The engine compartment, with no suggestion of fragility about the transmission or rear suspension. The complicated exhausts gave a clear 'racing' note, with none of the lumpy sounds characteristic of other race-tuned American V8s.

adhesive techniques). The doors were deeply cut into the roof line to provide easy entry and exit – in this context, the term 'easy' is relative! – but did not always fit well, or stay closed in the early days.

The suspension followed Lola lines and was conventional by contemporary mid-engined standards: double wishbones, angled to provide an anti-dive quality, coil spring/shock absorbers and anti-roll bar at the front; double trailing arms, transverse top links and lower wishbones, coil spring/shock absorbers and anti-roll bar at the rear. The mounting points were spread as far as possible to minimize local loadings, but the problems this could pose in wheel alignment geometry and local circuit tuning were a worry. So a computer was substituted for the art of a man like

Broadley, and in Ford terms probably speeded the design phase.

During Monza trials with the Lola and at the 1964 Le Mans test weekend, drivers reported rear-end instability, and Lunn was convinced this resulted from shortcomings in the rear suspension, that the problem was not an aerodynamic one. In fact, the car was developing an unhealthy amount of lift, which had been suggested during a series of wind-tunnel tests with scale models at Maryland University, and later in Ford's Dearborn tunnel with a full-size model. However, these tests were more concerned with the airflow to radiators and the engine compartment, engine air supply and cockpit ventilation. The scale model tests also led to anti-dive and anti-squat being introduced into the suspension; spoilers

John Wyer, Eric Broadley and Roy Lunn with their sleek new car before it was flown to New York for its presentation to the press in April 1964.

Britain's major international airline made capital out of flying the first FAV-built car across the Atlantic. It had single headlamps recessed into the nose panel, augmented by twin lights beneath the nose.

under the nose would seemingly cure any aerodynamic lift problems.

Practical experiments at the MIRA high-speed circuit proved the value of a rear spoiler, lift being converted to downforce with no drag penalty when a 4½in spoiler was fitted; in terms of stability the car was transformed, although curing the problems at the rear revealed a much less serious nose lift problem. It was left to Lunn to sum up the problem

most aptly, likening the car without a rear spoiler to an arrow without feathers. With 'feathers' in the form of a spoiler fitted, the problem was solved . . .

Brakes were outboard all round, initially with solid 11½in diameter cast-iron discs and Girling calipers. In 1964 races, the brakes overheated seriously and ventilated discs were introduced. There were no servos, separate master-cylinders were used for front and rear,

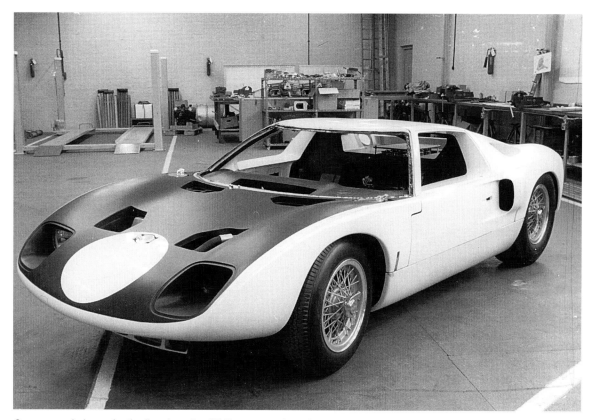

Seen as a whole car for the first time, the GT40 was stunning – just think of its contemporaries early in 1964. Here, GT101 awaits the glaziers and cockpit furnishers.

and a balance system allowed braking bias to be adjusted. The rack-and-pinion steering (2½ turns lock to lock) was mounted ahead of the footwell. The first cars were fitted with 15in Borrani wire wheels with alloy rims (6½in wide at the front, 8in at the rear), as it was felt that better brake cooling would be achieved, and in any case the proposed cast-magnesium wheels were not ready. There was to be a return to the handsome wire wheels in an open version and the later Mk III cars. Dunlop tyres were used in the first season, Goodyears thereafter.

The side sponsons were extended rearward from the cockpit area to support the engine, which did not have a load-bearing role. The V8 was the 4.2-litre (256cu in) unit which had been developed for the Indianapolis programme in 1963 and was a lightweight (aluminium block and heads, dry-sump) derivative of the 289cu in Fairlane engine. Its stock origins were suggested by its pushrod valve operation. (Plans to fit the dohc unit

under development for the 1964 Indianapolis programme in later cars were overtaken by a policy change, and this pure racing unit was seen only in later private conversions.) Four downdraught twin-choke Weber carburettors were used. The exhausts led to four-into-one collectors above the final drive and to a pair of final pipes. The engine was detuned from its Indianapolis form to run on commercially-available fuel, and there were other detail changes (for example, to the induction to give greater flexibility). An alternator and starter system were obvious additions, but just before the GT's Le Mans baptism the alternator was replaced by a dynamo as an insurance (there was to be a reversion to an alternator, and vibrations meant that it was to be a weakness, until owners learned to use rubber mountings). In this form, the V8 gave 350bhp at 7,200rpm, or around 83bhp/litre, with a maximum torque figure of 275lb.ft at 5,600rpm.

Transmission was through a Borg and Beck

In its earliest form the GT40 looked particularly neat in side elevation, with its smoothly contoured tail complementing the fine lines of the nose. Rear brake and engine cooling ducts were neatly integrated into the overall shape.

twin-plate clutch and Colotti Type 37 gearbox. This had four speeds and no synchromesh, but was felt to be the only box available if the construction schedule was to be maintained. However, some members of the team doubted whether it was up to the job of transmitting 350bhp through an endurance race, and have since claimed that the possibility that ZF could have supplied gearboxes in 1964 was not pursued – an unfortunate oversight, since the fragility of the Colotti unit was to become only too obvious. As a palliative in 1964, some Colotti straight-cut gears were to be replaced with Ford helical gears, but after two 1965 races ZF gearboxes were to be used. The transaxle package was completed with a straight-bevel final-drive gear, limited-slip differential and exposed drive-shafts. These had Cardan universal joints at the outer ends, while the original inboard pot joints soon gave way to bulky rubber 'doughnuts', to absorb torque reversals better and damp out harshness in the driveline, then to Dana couplings. The full-width opening rear bodywork gave first-class access to engine and transmission.

An elaborate ducting system took air from a pressure area under the nose to the cockpit and engine compartment (via ducts in the doors, while carburettor air was taken in directly just behind the doors). The ducting proved to be a most unwelcome built-in drag factor, as this aspect had not been taken into account – or investigation was not feasible – with the ⅜-scale model used for the wind-tunnel tests, where in any case really high-speed behaviour had to be extrapolated as the tunnel used had a top scale limit of 125mph.

In theory, the through-flow ventilation should have been adequate for the cockpit – the extractor vents were even arranged to draw some air through the seats – but in practice the early cockpits could get very hot. The driver's seat was fixed, with the pedals mounted on a cast-alloy member which could be adjusted to suit drivers of varying heights, and at first even the seat back was inflatable to allow for additional tiny personal requirements. Generally, the driving position was good . . . and something Dallara might have looked at carefully when he laid out the Lamborghini Miura . . .

The car was well received in New York by a press which included elements prepared to be hostile, and that was important to Ford. To that extent, the digression outweighed the loss of four days when testing time was precious. The second car was completed 10 days after the first, but bad weather meant that there was time for no more than bedding-in runs totalling four hours (426 miles) before the two cars were rushed to France for the GT's first public appearance at the Le Mans test weekend.

3

Lessons at Le Mans

1964 and a change of direction

Le Mans was wet and cold in mid-April 1964 – daunting conditions for a new team about to run its new cars on a fast circuit for the first time. Moreover, Ferrari rose to the challenge, with cars ready to go as soon as the circuit was closed and while it was no more than damp. Lodovico Scarfiotti set the target by lapping in 4min 43.8sec (134.55mph, 216.53km/h) in a 3.3-litre 275P, while John Surtees was timed at 194mph, 312km/h in a 4-litre 330P on the Mulsanne straight.

The Fords were late out, and the team very soon became aware of the seriousness of the instability problem: drivers could not use full revs in top gear. Worse was to come as Jo Schlesser crashed at the kink in the Mulsanne straight at an estimated 150mph, and the car was seriously damaged. Next day, Roy Salvadori crashed in the braking area at the end of the straight. He had gone to the weekend with misgivings about the car, and these seemed to be confirmed as he worked it up to speed, especially on the Mulsanne straight, where gusting winds aggravated handling problems. Moreover, he was perhaps the first driver to experience the shock of a GT40 door opening at high speed. He was being careful when he crashed, but although the car was only slightly damaged, it could not be used again that weekend, so little was learned about the all-important aspect of fuel consumption at Le Mans.

At least the weekend led to hard thinking about aerodynamics, and in a discussion between Wyer, Lunn and the drivers, misgivings about a rear spoiler were set aside. MIRA tests showed just how effective it was, transforming the car and giving drivers a great confidence boost.

At Le Mans in April, the best Ford laps had been 13th fastest (Schlesser, 4min 21.8sec) and 21st fastest (Salvadori, 4min 35.7sec), while the best straight-line speed was well below the theoretical maximum at 174mph, 280km/h, because of the self-imposed rev limitation.

The team had to learn, and they entered a car for the Nürburgring 1,000kms on May 31 for a test under racing conditions before Le Mans. The drivers were the vastly-experienced pair of Phil Hill and Bruce McLaren (the New Zealander had undertaken much of the development driving, including the MIRA aerodynamic work with Roy Salvadori, who then left the team). On the face of it, the car performed well in Germany. Hill qualified second fastest in 9min 04.7sec – under the existing sportscar lap record (but Surtees was almost six seconds faster still). The Ford was second at the end of the first lap, then lost two places, but it kept in touch with the leading trio of Ferraris. McLaren held this place only briefly after the routine stop at 11 laps, then slowed with gear selector problems and retired after 15 laps. The specific cause of retirement was a weld failure in a rear suspension mounting point, but although pounding round the demanding Nürburgring had shown up

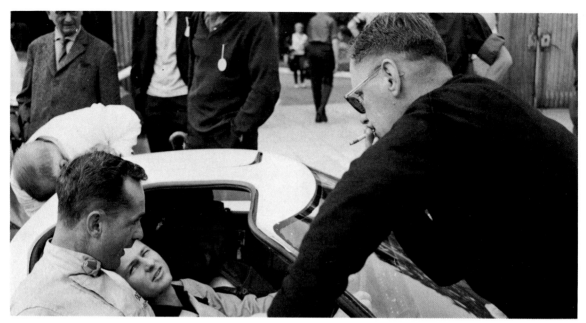

Phil Hill and Bruce McLaren (in the cockpit, *above*) at the Nürburgring before practice for the GT40's first race. The extent to which the doors were cut into the roof is clearly shown in the lower picture as Hill prepares to go out on the circuit. The doors were sometimes reluctant to stay closed. The twin scuttle intakes have been blanked off; NACA intakes for cockpit air were to appear in 1965.

The GT40's racing career began in exuberant style as Phil Hill fought to control a vicious tail slide as he accelerated away from a Le Mans-type start at the Nürburgring.

Hill also had the tail well out through the South Curve as he grappled for grip alongside a Cobra and a Ferrari LM through the long right-hander. Lesser drivers were to find the practice a little hazardous!

The incorporation of all the headlamps within the wings and the addition of a tail spoiler were the most obvious changes from the first FAV-built car. This shot of 102 at the Nürburgring emphasizes the elegant lines of the GT40. The revised tail was immediately effective and its profile was to remain unchanged through the GT40's life.

weaknesses in welds – more than one was failing – that weakness had also served to disguise shortcomings in the transmission. However, the car's true potential had been demonstrated . . .

Three works Fords, still GTs, number 102 (the Nürburgring car) and the slightly lighter 103 and 104, were presented for scrutineering at Le Mans for their first entry in the race that was the main reason for their existence. There were problems – displacement blocks had to be used to reduce fuel tank capacity to the permitted 140 litres – while the constant presence of a Ford contingent brought some discomfort to the working members of the team.

John Wyer was realistic about the team's chances and made it clear that he would have preferred a quiet baptism of fire at Le Mans, that he would have liked some of the Ford people to just go away (it should be remembered that the operation of the team was largely along British 'gentlemen and

amateurs' lines, and the professionalism of some Ford personnel such as PR men was alien).

Actual practice was very encouraging, especially after the poor showing in April. The five fastest times on the first day were set by Ferrari drivers, but Ginther and McLaren lapped in under four minutes and the American was timed at 192mph, 309km/h, on the Mulsanne straight. This was close to the theoretical still-air potential maximum speed of the early car of 197mph, 317km/h (this in turn was below the original design estimate of around 210mph, 338km/h, because of unallowed-for drag, for some of the ducting had no clear outlet for the air taken in, and so this much-lauded system absorbed 76bhp rather than the estimated 30bhp).

On the second day, John Surtees lapped in 3min 42sec (135.64mph, 218.28km/h) in a 4-litre Ferrari 330P, and Richie Ginther responded with a time of 3min 45.3sec. Six cars recorded times under the existing lap

Verification at Le Mans before Ford's first assault on the 24-hour race. *Above:* John Wyer deals with officials while Ford's Harry Calton, with crossed arms, tries to look unperturbed behind the car. *Below:* The chaps creeping about under GT102 appear to be scrutineers . . .

record of 3min 53.3sec, which stood to Surtees, four Ferraris and two Fords: the Ginther/Gregory Ford was second fastest and the Hill/McLaren car fourth fastest. The third Ford, driven by Attwood and Schlesser, was only just outside the record.

The promise of a Ferrari-Ford battle attracted an enormous crowd, and through the daylight hours of June 20 they saw that promise fulfilled. On the second lap, Ginther passed three Ferraris to lead the race, leap-frogging from Ferrari tow to Ferrari tow on the Mulsanne straight and seeing 7,200rpm before braking (and that suggested he had exceeded 200mph).

Ginther increased his lead convincingly for 1½ hours, when he stopped to hand over to Masten Gregory – at 15 laps the Ford was 40 seconds ahead of Surtees' Ferrari in second

place. But the separate fuel tanks of the Ford meant that its stop was long, and when Gregory returned to the race the positions were almost precisely reversed. The Ford held second place into the evening, but during the fifth hour it was retired with gearbox selector failure.

The Attwood/Schlesser car had run as high as sixth in the third and fourth hours, at a controlled rather than a challenging pace, then it caught fire: a nylon fuel hose had been used instead of the specified armoured hose and it had split, allowing fuel to leak.

Phil Hill got away sluggishly at the start, and five pit stops in the first hour dropped this car to 44th place. Eventually, the misfire was traced to carburation, and once the car was running healthily Hill and McLaren worked it up the order, to sixth place after eight hours

Above: Richie Ginther accelerates out of Tertre Rouge at Le Mans in 1964 in pursuit of John Surtees' Ferrari. This GT40 (103) led the race in its early stages. *Below:* Richard Attwood in the car that was destined to catch fire when leaking fuel spilt as he accelerated out of Mulsanne corner; the driver escaped unhurt. All three Fords were equipped with nose spoilers and – interestingly – bug deflectors ahead of the windscreen.

31

and to fourth before it retired after 13½ hours. Early in the morning, Hill set a new lap record of 3min 39.4sec (131.42mph, 211.49km/h).

Success first time out at Le Mans was by no means unknown, notwithstanding an old adage that three years were needed to develop a Le Mans winner. For a car with little development behind it the GT had performed well – not well enough for some Ford executives, but well by any other standard, and the main weakness had been in bought-in components, for which there was no instant cure. Be that as it may, the new man from head office, Leo Beebe, perceived that the GT effort had to be restructured, and firm control returned to Dearborn. Meanwhile, there was to be one more major team effort in 1964, in the 12-hour race at Reims, early in July.

That left little time to refettle the cars after Le Mans, but the gearboxes had new Ford selectors, and a new car (105) was fitted with the Shelby-developed Cobra engine. This 4.7-litre V8 was based on the 289cu in Fairlane iron-block unit which, unlike the Indianapolis engine, had a shallow wet sump, with baffles

to take care of an oil surge problem. It weighed only a little more than the light-alloy engine – Ford's foundry techniques were first class – and in its installation in the GT40 the elimination of a front-mounted oil radiator and associated plumbing meant that there was a small weight saving as well. Meanwhile, at Reims, the 41lb penalty was hardly significant and the car proved equally competitive with this engine (it was rated at 370bhp at 6,700rpm, with more torque low down than the Indianapolis engine, which should have been an advantage with the Colotti box).

The team's achievement was similar to Le Mans – three retirements with another lap record as meagre consolation. The bonus of Fords battling against Ferraris was diluted, for although Ginther and McLaren stayed with the leaders during the opening phase, they then fell away. The transmission in Ginther's car failed, then at dawn the transmission in the Attwood/Schlesser car also failed, after a drain plug had fallen out and the loss of oil had damaged the gearbox. The crankshaft broke in the McLaren/Hill car, although it

A formidable package. This is the 7-litre Ford 427 engine and substantial transaxle assembly as fitted to the Mk II. Power output was quoted as 485bhp at 6,200rpm and maximum torque as around 475lb.ft at 5,000rpm.

The massive rear end of the first of the 7-litre cars, that were to become known as Mk IIs. By this time race tyres were moving from the conventionally treaded type towards slicks.

suited Ford's book to put about a story that this retirement, too, resulted from transmission failure.

There was just one more outing in 1964, when two cars with 289 engines were sent to the Nassau Speed Week. That was an odd decision, suggesting that some people at Dearborn still did not fully appreciate the branch of the sport in which Ford had become involved: there had been further tests at Monza in the early autumn, and if the intention was to race-prove that work then a duration event like the 1,000km race at Montlhéry in October would have been appropriate. The Bahamas week, with its main event the 252-mile Nassau Trophy on a twisty little circuit ideal for the sports-racing cars that made up the bulk of the entry, was not suited to cars like the Fords. Front suspension failures put both cars out early in the proceedings – the worst result so far in the Ford programme.

Leo Beebe had taken over the Special Vehicles Activity from Frank Zimmerman in May and, with his first-hand experience concentrated on the Le Mans race, had started to reshape the programme. In corporate terms a shake-out, perhaps, seemed more sensible than a refinement of an existing operation, or at least could be presented as more progressive. Time was to show that the GT40 could be developed into a race-winning car, at a relatively low cost. Immediately, though, the new programme aimed at the 1965 Le Mans race was to cost some $4.5 million (roughly double the 1964 cost) and it was to be no more successful, in part because it repeated the mistake of going to the race with under-developed cars. The side benefits from the changes, however, were to be considerable.

The first of these was that the GT40 was to be put into production by Ford Advanced Vehicles in Slough. Under John Wyer, FAV would also supply base cars and components for the US-centred racing operation and would enter cars in races in its own name. The production GT40 specification, frozen in June 1965, included the five-speed ZF transaxle and the 289 engine. Eric Broadley had not been a happy member of the FAV team and bowed out at that point, regaining his independence and resuming his Lola activities (next door to FAV!).

Roy Lunn and his engineering team returned to the USA to set up shop in another Ford acquisition, Kar Kraft, whose small specialist plant was physically similar to the FAV factory, with offices and an assembly shop. It was some four miles from the main Dearborn factory – suffciently remote for it to avoid artificial cost overheads and trade union regulations, although the small permanent staff was backed by Ford 'moonlighters'.

The administration of the official racing programme, together with some development work and of course race preparation, became the responsibility of Carroll Shelby. He had a good record as a driver (ironically, one of his successes had been at Le Mans in 1959, as a member of the Aston Martin team then run by John Wyer) and he had made a great success of the Cobra. This marriage between an AC chassis and American V8 power had been his inspiration, and in time its coupe version – evolved without the aid of wind-tunnels or computers – proved more than a match for more sophisticated race-bred GT Ferraris. At first, Cobras had a 'Powered by Ford' label, but eventually they became 'Fords' and in some measure they made up for 1964-65 disappointments when they won the GT Championship in 1965, the first-ever international championship to fall to an American manufacturer.

Shelby American was located in the one-time Reventlow plant at Venice, Los Angeles, and among its personnel were Phil Remington, a 'natural' automotive engineer who had also been involved in the Ford Indianapolis programme and had worked at Slough on the first GTs, and Ken Miles, an expatriate Englishman and a gifted development driver. Ford's Aeronutronic company provided some back up, bringing aerospace techniques to the analysis of aerodynamic and roadholding problems. In these areas Remington reworked the infamous ducting (along the way the seat cooling arrangement, which had proved to have about as much value as cosmetic chrome, was discarded), while practical circuit work established that modifications to the original suspension settings had improved things worse!

The 289 engine was standardized (in any case there had been a shortage of

Long-nosed 7-litre 106 being driven by Bruce McLaren during practice at Le Mans in 1965. The two Shelby cars still had the original colour scheme, with a matt-painted top to the nose.

The first roadster GT40 (108) on test in England early in 1965. In place of intakes on the flanks, this car has neat intakes above the level of the wheelarches. Although it has a tail spoiler, there is no nose spoiler.

'Indianapolis' V8s, and by the end of the year most had cracked blocks); pending the arrival of new ZF gearboxes, some 21 changes were made to the transaxle; and cast-alloy wheels (8in front rims, 9½in rear rims) and wider Goodyears were introduced. The cars were repainted in Shelby's colours – dark blue, with two white stripes running nose-to-tail on the centre line. Two cars were ready for the 2,000km Daytona Continental race at the end of February 1965.

While Shelby worked to achieve reliability and raceworthiness in the mainline racing GTs, FAV was working towards GT40 production. Len Bailey revised the nose lines, achieving a worthwhile reduction in drag, and construction of a first open car was started. This was on traditional 'spyder' lines, and one objective was to facilitate direct comparison with the normal coupe version.

A feeling that time had already caught up with the GT prevailed at Kar Kraft, where Roy Lunn's team was developing the prototype which was to become the Mk II. Power-to-weight had become a preoccupation, and project studies looked into two main possibilities – obtaining more power from the 4.7-litre (289) engine or using an adaptation of a 7-litre (427cu in) V8. The smaller engine was eventually to be developed to produce 390bhp at 7,000rpm, and an enlarged version was feasible, but the emphasis swung to the 427 unit.

This was the Galaxie V8, which had been developed for stock car racing to give around 525bhp and had proved reliable. It was not a thoroughbred engine, it was heavy (600lb), in terms of outright power for its capacity it was not notably efficient, and its use would involve the development of a new driveline. But it was felt that the advantages outweighed the drawbacks, and the decision was made to go ahead with a prototype. Detuned for its new use, the engine gave some 427bhp at only 6,200rpm, with tremendous torque, so engine work was concentrated on achieving durability.

Little modification was needed to actually fit it into the GT40 (the rear bulkhead was adjusted), while the nose had to be changed to accommodate a larger radiator and oil tank. A new heavy-duty transmission was devised, expediency meaning that the Galaxie gear cluster and shafts were used in a light-alloy casing – here again developed and tried components were expected to offset the weight and a degree of inefficiency that resulted from humble origins. In other respects, such as suspension, GT components were carried over virtually unchanged to the new car.

Through the winter of 1964-65, the intention was to build a test vehicle for comparative evaluation. The first Mk II (so designated only in retrospect, but here conveniently referred to as such) was completed in April 1965, and first run on a handling test track. It was then taken to Ford's high-speed oval at Romeo (Michigan), where it lapped at 180mph in the first session. After aerodynamic adjustments, Miles took it out and lapped at 201.5mph, exceeding 210mph on the straight. Handling was good, not quite at par with a well set up GT, but then those first cars could never have achieved lap speeds approaching 180mph, let alone in excess of 200mph.

Extrapolating the Romeo test figures, Lunn's group calculated that the 427 car could lap Le Mans in under 3min 35sec without ever exceeding 6,200rpm. The aim had been to run the development programme with a view to racing the Mk II in 1966; now Ford was encouraged to race it at Le Mans in 1965, despite the fact that it could not be tried at the test weekend. The first car was stripped and rebuilt after its crash test programme, a second was hastily built, and the pair was sent to France.

Meanwhile, FAV had completed a second open car in time for the mid-April test days at Le Mans. Around the cockpit, the roadster was reminiscent of contemporary P2 Ferraris, even to an aerodynamic roll-over structure behind the cockpit, while the nose lines were not enhanced by a large air intake (primarily for the brakes). A five-speed all-synchro ZF gearbox was used and the attractive wire wheels were retained. The open GT40 was lighter, but stiffness was considerably reduced, there was no aerodynamic advantage and drivers complained of buffeting. These drawbacks could have been overcome, and were in the open Mk V many years later; from a viewpoint in the 1990s it seems a pity that the original roadster GT40 was abandoned . . .

4

A Season of Setbacks
1965 and the first Mk IIs

Early in 1965, the whole endeavour was given a much-needed fillip – a race victory. The entry for the 2,000km Daytona Continental was not strong, but it did include a Ferrari 330P2, a works car in all but name, driven by Surtees and Rodriguez, a NART Ferrari and Dan Gurney's ever-fragile Lotus 19, fitted with a 326 (5.3-litre) version of the 289 engine, producing an estimated 420bhp. This car was to be the hare. Rodriguez was fastest in practice in the P2, but the two Shelby Fords were second and third, their drivers permitted to use 6,500rpm in qualifying, although a 6,000rpm restriction was applied in the race. There was also concern about the durability of the new Kelsey-Hayes ventilated disc brakes, and these had to be replaced by 1964-pattern Girlings.

Gurney led off as expected, the NART Ferrari blew a tyre at speed and was retired, and so did the P2 approaching quarter-distance. When the engine of the Lotus failed, the two Fords were left to head a flock of Cobras. Ken Miles and Lloyd Ruby won at 99.94mph (160.80km/h), but the Ginther /Bondurant car fell away through the second half of the race, losing time with a starter problem at each pit stop, and finished third.

Prospects at Sebring for the 12-hour race were discouraging for Ford. The Ferrari presence was not strong, but the Chaparral lightweight sports-racers were accepted for the race, and in too many minds Chaparral was associated with General Motors . . .

Fractions of a second in practice laps for an endurance race mean little, but the Hall/Sharp Chaparral was 10 seconds faster than the best Ford. Gurney – running his Lotus in Shelby colours – led briefly as Hall made the first Chaparral pit stop, but once the Lotus had retired the Chaparral was unchallenged (Sharp was even able to sit out the worst of a downpour in the pits). Ginther's Ford retired with rear suspension failure, but McLaren and Miles finished second, four laps behind the Chaparral, and won the GT Prototype category.

The focus of attention shifted to Europe, where the Fords could be expected to face Ferrari in full strength. At the Le Mans test weekend, early in April, there were only four Fords, the Shelby pair which had been run at Daytona and Sebring, the FAV open car and a coupe run in the name of Ford France. All had 4.7-litre engines, the Shelby cars with Colotti Type 37 gearboxes, while the two from FAV were fitted with ZF gearboxes. One of the Shelby cars ran with a long nose, intended to improve penetration, and was soon fitted with spoilers in an attempt to cure lift at speed. In detail, the FAV cars had revised carburation and exhausts.

It was a weekend when Ferrari set the pace and the Ford teams got in mileage. Surtees carved no less than 14.1 seconds from the lap record with a shattering 3min 35.1sec lap in a 330P2. Attwood was the fastest Ford driver (in 3min 40.9sec), while Whitmore got down to

First victory. *Above:* The Miles/Ruby GT40 being closely followed by the Ginther/Bondurant sister car at Daytona in 1965, both Fords running in Shelby colours. *Below:* Ken Miles, in the winning car, alongside Walt Hansgen's Ferrari on the Daytona banking.

Sir John Whitmore at the 1965 Le Mans test weekend with the FAV open GT40 (111) when the car was fitted with nose spoilers beneath the lights.

3min 44.9sec in a coupe and 3min 50.0sec in the open car, and Bob Bondurant lapped in 3min 42.9sec for Shelby.

At Monza, for the 1,000km race over the combined circuit, the two Shelby cars were never in the hunt, although Ferraris were the first cars to suffer on the bumpy concrete of the banked part of the track. Ferraris finished first and second, but McLaren and Miles drove one of the Fords through to a first European finish, in third place. The other Ford, driven by Amon and Maglioli, retired with collapsed front suspension.

FAV sent its open car painted in a curiously light green to Sicily for the Targa Florio, it seems with scant preparation and insufficient spares. It misfired through the first lap, then lost a wheel on the third. Whitmore fitted the spare and got the car back to the pits, but four laps later Bondurant lost control on gravel which another driver had spread across the road and wiped off a front wheel and suspension on Sicilian stone.

Four Fords turned out at the Nürburgring for the race that marked the anniversary of the car's debut. One of the Shelby cars had a 5.3-litre (325cu in) engine for this race, which mangled drive-shafts in practice and in the race. Amon started in the other blue car and, despite a misfire, ran in third place during the opening phase. Then he missed a pit signal, ran out of fuel short of the pits on his 'extra' lap, and had to push the car a kilometre for McLaren to take over. Bruce restarted 21st, and at the end the car had been worked back up to eighth place. Attwood and Whitmore also ran as high as third in the open FAV car, retiring when an engine mounting broke. A similar failure accounted for Ligier's Ford France entry (1003) driven by Trintignant and Ligier.

Quite incidentally to the main theme, a GT40 raced for the first time on a British circuit, Attwood taking fifth place in a minor

Bob Bondurant at the wheel of the open GT40 during the 1965 Targa Florio, when he shared the car with Sir John Whitmore. It was retired with front-end damage after Bondurant slid on gravel. This is 111 again, but painted green since the Le Mans tests and with a transverse lip ahead of the radiator air outlets.

event at Silverstone, then finishing second in a Guards Trophy race at Mallory Park (Salvadori later drove the same car, 1002, owned by F English, to a second place at Goodwood).

For Ford, the main-line European events had been an overture to Le Mans, and there had been rather too many discordant notes. One way to change the odds was to use more cubic inches, but there were now misgivings that too much time had already been devoted to 'Indianapolis' engine development and too little to the Mk II; another way was thought to lie in numbers, so late in the day John Wyer was asked to arrange more entries. He persuaded Rob Walker and Georges Filipinetti to change their accepted entries of Ferraris to

Shelby Fords and, as importantly, persuaded the ACO to accept the changes. These two cars were to be run by Shelby American, which in addition to the lead pair of Mk IIs was also running two of the Cobras in the race. Foresight might have suggested that the additional entries could have faired better under the wing of FAV, for Shelby and his racing manager Carroll Smith had little experience of running a team in major European events, and the extra load could well prove too great for them, even though the assistance of a large Ford entourage was available. All the while, vastly experienced team managers were on hand, and were largely ignored . . .

The FAV entry was its last in a European

race, although its development car, 105, was to be run at Daytona and Sebring in 1966. The car provided for Ford France at Le Mans was a roadster completed by Shelby (109), which differed in detail from the FAV open cars.

One sign of change was to be seen in the many mechanics wearing smart overalls in team colours (or uniform orange weatherproofs when it rained), at a time when nondescript gear was still the European norm.

To add to the administrative problems, some of the cars were hardly ready. Neither of the Mk IIs had run at a race circuit – the second of them had not turned a wheel before it was sent to France – and the first official practice session had to be devoted to setting them up. Something was relearned about high-speed aerodynamics as a rear spoiler and stabilizing fins were added, then a nose spoiler to achieve balance was extemporized and nose strakes were also added. With these aids, and when the rear anti-roll bar was dispensed with, the big cars became well-mannered; near the end of practice, Shelby asked Phil Hill to set a time Ferrari could not match, and Hill

turned in a lap in 3min 33.0sec in the newest Mk II – 141.4mph (227.5km/h), with an estimated maximum speed of 213mph (343km/h) on the Mulsanne straight. He observed the rev limit, and had to hold first gear in. His time was within Lunn's 3:30-3:35 calculations, and it was very much better than Surtees' 3min 38.1sec in a 4-litre Ferrari 330P2. Miles lapped in the other Mk II in 3min 38.9sec, a fraction slower than Bondurant's 3min 38.7sec in the Walker car.

The 7-litre engines did not behave impeccably – they had yet to be developed as endurance racing power units – but more worries were caused by differentials and gearboxes (and in all the vast collection of Ford spare parts there was apparently only one spare gearbox!). Fuel consumption was to be established during the opening hours of the race, and refuelling times measured at the first pit stops . . .

There were also misgivings about the 5.3-litre engines in the Walker and Filipinetti cars, and these were changed for 4.7-litre V8s after practice (the FAV and Ford France GT40s ran

Leo Beebe and Ray Geddes in the Ford garage at Le Mans. The stripped GT40 behind them was the Bondurant/Maglioli race car, while the Cobra Daytona Coupe alongside it was driven by Gurney and Grant. None of the Fords and only one Cobra survived the 24 hours.

The first 7-litre car (106) at Le Mans in 1965. The chin spoiler is obviously a hasty addition to an otherwise immaculate car. It was one of the first pair with the 427 engine and Kar Kraft four-speed transaxle. The Mk II designation was to come later.

In the 1965 Le Mans race, the 7-litre cars ran with smaller front spoilers, but with strakes ahead of the front wheelarches, and stabilizing fins and a transverse spoiler at the rear. The larger intake and single radiator air outlet are distinctive.

One of the Le Mans Mk IIs on the morning of the race. Note the ducting between the suspension top mounts and the rear brakes, also the way in which the necessarily complicated exhaust system has been routed as tidily as possible.

throughout with the smaller engines). John Wyer set a 3min 55sec lap target for the FAV car, closely estimating the speed at which the race would be run, but the smaller engines had cylinder head faults, overheating at over 6,000rpm, so these cars failed to match the 1964 straight-line speeds. In the race, the two Shelby cars being run in the names of Walker and Filipinetti retired during the second hour with cylinder head gasket failures.

From the start, the blue and white 7-litre cars set the pace, McLaren and Amon leading the Ferraris driven by Surtees and Guichet in the opening phase. McLaren set a 3min 45.2sec record on the first flying lap, and three laps later Chris Amon set the new record for the circuit at 3min 37.7sec (138.22mph, 222.39km/h). The lead pair ran almost nose-to-tail, and drew away from the Ferraris at around five seconds a lap – as in 1964, Ford got value from the opening phase of the 24-hour race.

Car 106 at Le Mans in 1965 again, this view showing the extemporized tail spoiler as well as the fins. Driven by Bruce McLaren and Ken Miles, it led the race in its early hours, but was destined to retire with transmission trouble before dusk on Saturday.

This was the FAV entry for Le Mans in 1965, fitted with the definitive GT40 nose. It was driven by Innes Ireland and Sir John Whitmore. Overheating caused its retirement in the sixth hour.

The one-off X-1, which was raced in four events late in 1965, without success. Here it is being driven by Chris Amon in its first race, the Canadian GP at Mosport Park, when it had a full set of lights. Colours followed the main-line GT40s.

After the first refuelling stop, in little over an hour, McLaren still led the Ferraris. But the new car stopped for 38 minutes, Hill taking over from Amon and restarting in 35th place after work on the clutch and gearbox. In the fourth hour the McLaren-Miles car retired with transmission failure.

The Ford France car had retired early, ironically when its ZF gearbox failed; the FAV car lasted into the sixth hour before it was retired, extravagantly overheating as the cylinder head gasket failed. That left the newest

of the Fords racing on into the night. But by midnight the Ford effort had collapsed, totally: the transmission in the second Mk II failed, like the first because of poor final preparation (dirt in the clutch slave cylinder in one case, the use of a reject gear in the other). The works Ferraris all retired during Sunday morning, leaving victory to the independent North American Racing Team 3.3-litre Ferrari 250LM. Four of the five Cobras which had been regarded as a Ford back-up also retired, the AC-entered car driven by Jack Sears and Dick

The X-1, which again has Amon at the wheel, in action at Riverside, where it had a revised nose, without lights, and some minor aerodynamic variations. A GT40 tail had air intakes reminiscent of the FAV open GT40.

Shelby ran this car (104) at the 1965 Le Mans test weekend, when it was driven by Bob Bondurant. Its experimental nose was fitted over the existing bodywork; weight distribution and handling were adversely affected and there were no apparent benefits.

Thompson finishing an unimpressive eighth.

Ford withdrew from the Reims 12-hour race, and their people went their separate ways after Le Mans. Once a brief spasm of uncertainty at Dearborn had passed, FAV continued GT40 production, the objective being to complete 50 cars before the end of the year in order to qualify the GT40 as a Group 4 competition car for the World Championship of Makes in 1966, and also got down to some sensible development work.

Dearborn polemics could have had far-reaching consequences, but while one management faction did argue for the closure of the whole operation, the conclusion once shock waves had passed was that the Le Mans debacle need not be terminal. To a degree it had resulted from self-inflicted wounds – the mechanical failings had not been fundamental, but had stemmed from preparation that was less than thorough. The major faults in the executive approach to the race were recognized, too, and this time the lessons were applied. Despite its failure, the Mk II way was obviously the right way to go for 1966 – basically, to exploit the virtues of lots of lazily-revving litres.

John Cowley, who had been involved in a NASCAR programme in the early 1960s, became Ford's racing manager, and more expertise was brought in, notably Holman & Moody from the stock car world. A committee

with the power to cut through red tape was set up, one of its first tasks being to ensure that the programme was rationalized, and that all the participants pulled in the same direction.

The 1965 season ended with modest success, too, when Peter Sutcliffe took a GT40 to South Africa to win a three-hour race and, with Innes Ireland co-driving, to finish second to a Ferrari 365P in the Kyalami Nine Hours.

The X-1 Group 7 sports-racing derivative was built by Bruce McLaren Motor Racing, and was a worthwhile development contract for that small outfit. The basis was a lightweight chassis by Abbey Panels, and it was numbered (110) among the first-series cars. An open car, it had the long nose of the original Mk II, which looked sleeker once the main lights were removed, save that aerodynamic appendages were added. It was intended to contribute to Mk II development, and to this end it was run with an automatic transmission after it had been raced with a Hewland manual gearbox. It was to be rebuilt as a Mk II by Kar Kraft, still as a roadster.

In Group 7 racing its weight told against it and it recorded only one finish – fifth in the *Times* Grand Prix at Riverside. As a Mk II it was run by Shelby American, and driven by Miles and Ruby to win the 1966 Sebring 12-hour race. Ford was later to flirt with another sports-racing spin-off from the main programme, but with no more success.

5

Developing the Mk II

The 'lazy litres' approach

One of the major objectives of 'Total Performance' – victory at Indianapolis – had been secured in 1965, and Ford's racing advocates could therefore focus clearly on Le Mans in 1966. There was a new management structure, which could be seen as a recipe for big-corporation decision-by-committee muddles by people accustomed to tight-knit racing teams, where dictatorship is more effective than democracy. But in Ford's case the harsh experiences of the 24-hour races in 1964-65 had brought a new sense of reality, and this led to co-ordinated efforts. This committee system worked.

Ford Division Vice-President Donald Frey, who as General Manager had negotiated with Ferrari, carried the prime responsibility, while Leo Beebe was director of racing. Jacque Passino was manager of the Special Vehicles Activity, covering all high-performance cars, and John Cowley was race director, with Homer Perry and Chuck Folger as his lieutenants. The Le Mans committee included members of the divisions which had some involvement, such as Engine and Foundry, Transmission and Chassis. Kar Kraft, under Roy Lunn, continued its design and prototype build work, while three teams, Shelby American, Holman & Moody and Alan Mann Racing, were to test and develop, prepare and race cars: some friction resulted, especially between the two American outfits, but this was largely tolerated as a healthy spur. The spread of work among teams was not regarded as evidence of fragmentation, rather as evidence that the managing committee did not show favours.

Beyond that, Ford had flung a lot of money at the programme, and there was a determination that the job should now be done properly, for example in testing to the extent that each race should be 'rehearsed'.

Shelby American Inc and Alan Mann Racing also built up cars, the former working with cars or rolling chassis from FAV, while Mann's cars had more complex origins. Shelby's first two cars came from the pre-production series, and were completed as roadsters. The coupes were to be modified in many details, for example with repositioned oil coolers and their air intakes, and larger water radiators. Alternative engines were tried, and one car was raced with a 325 CID engine. There were minor bodywork variations, and Halibrand cast wheels were generally used as the wire wheels were not trusted.

The second Shelby pair came from the production series, and were prepared for independent entrants at Le Mans in 1965; they were then set aside, and both were eventually returned to FAV, where one was soon sold, but the other was eventually uprated to 1968 standard by JWA and raced again. After the 1965 Le Mans race, Shelby concentrated on the Mk II.

Two production cars were supplied to Alan Mann for development. However, they were used as a source of parts for Mann's

The requirement that an endurance racing car should be equipped to carry luggage often seemed a ludicrous throwback – provision to meet this regulation can be seen in the form of twin luggage boxes flanking the exhausts in the rear view of the Andretti/Bianchi Mk II at Le Mans in 1966.

lightweights (which was to lead to some confusion of chassis numbers). These lightweight cars were built around Abbey Panels-modified chassis, in which aluminium took the place of some steel. Aluminium body panels were used, the top of the cockpit was narrower, and the suspension was modified in detail – designer Len Bailey was later to recall these cars as forerunners of the Mirage derivative for which he was to be responsible a year later. These were numbered AM1 and AM2 (or AMR/1 and AMR/2, or AMGT-1 and AMGT-2), and had the 4.7-litre V8s driving through ZF five-speed gearboxes.

The pair showed promise at Sebring in 1965, but neither finished the race. At the Le Mans test weekend they were outpaced by the

Mk IIs, and Mann had one of these for the team's next race, the Spa 1000kms. However, the second of these cars was eventually bought by Paul Hawkins, who replaced the lightweight panels and restored the GT40 upper cockpit/roof lines to comply with Group 4 regulations. This red car was to become perhaps the most familiar private-entrant GT40, as Hawkins raced it very successfully in 1967-68.

However, the primary task for all concerned was to develop the Mk II, as it was officially designated by that time, and that involved extensive testing. The Dearborn wind-tunnel was used, but the emphasis on practical track work was much greater than in the early days, with the teams running cars at Daytona,

The 1966 Mk II could be distinguished by its shorter GT40-type nose, revised radiator air outlet, larger wheelarches and additional rear brake air intakes. This is Chris Amon at the wheel of the Le Mans-winning Shelby car, which he shared with Bruce McLaren – the black and silver New Zealand colours were wholly appropriate.

Riverside, Sebring and Ford's Arizona proving grounds. FAV carried out endurance tests at Monza, but these were intended to benefit GT40 customers rather than the main racing programme.

Two main engine dynamometer test programmes were run, primarily to prove durability; a wide-open throttle test was run over six hours at engine speeds up to 7,000rpm – well above the race restriction imposed on drivers – while another test simulated a Le Mans driving pattern for 48 hours, to allow for running-in and practice as well as the 24 hours of the race.

In another sideline, Ford of Britain took up the theme of 'added lightness' and a variant was developed by Len Bailey. However, this project was not carried through, and in that the 7-litre cars were to succeed there was never a need for it as back-up insurance. In any case, it was quite possible that any attempt to race it would have contravened inter-company and inter-team agreements and could have been subject to a Dearborn veto. However, the findings and some of the work done on it were carried forward, in part to the Mirage and then to the 3-litre prototypes built by Alan Mann to the 1968 regulations (Len Bailey was involved in all three cars).

'Added lightness' was reckoned to be an Alan Mann speciality, and that led to three Mk II offshoots carrying XGT designations, which were partly built by Mann's mechanics at the Shelby American plant. Two of these started at

The first J car nearing completion at the Kar Kraft plant near Dearborn, Michigan.

Le Mans in 1966 (the third was never raced), then when Mann's involvement with the programme ended the XGTs were retired.

The Mk II was raceworthy for the opening events of 1966. The chassis structure was little changed from the original, although engine and suspension mounting points were beefed-up. Outwardly, the most obvious change was at the front, with a reversion to the GT40 nose, 9in shorter than the first Mk II, lighter and aerodynamically efficient so that the tabs and spoilers which had to be added at Le Mans in 1965 were not needed (nor were the rear fins, and only the spoiler remained at the tail). Air intakes were added above the existing pair of scoops, on the line of the rear of the cockpit, for rear brake cooling, and ventilated discs were used all round.

The 1966 target power output for the 427 engine was 485bhp, hardly sensational in a world of sophisticated racing engines and not too difficult to achieve, so durability and weight reduction had priority. To the latter end, light-alloy cylinder heads and other parts had already been introduced and had brought a useful reduction in dry weight to 550lb, compared with the 600lb NASCAR 7-litre unit, but the extra weight of the new dry-sump arrangement meant that the 1966 version weighed only a few pounds less than 1965 Mk II engines. There were other modifications, for example to the Holley carburettor and in the use of three electric fuel pumps in place of mechanical units (two were connected in parallel, the third was an emergency or reserve pump).

Most of the arguments for using this heavy, unsophisticated and slow-revving engine seemed to be vindicated when it was pitted against 'pure-bred' racing units. It was flexible, so that a four-speed gearbox was adequate (it would pull in fourth from 1,000rpm), it was perhaps the least costly major component in the programme, and it was to become reliable. It was 'safe' to 7,400rpm, but a 6,200rpm restriction was applied in racing. By early summer most of the race units were delivering the target power – a few fell below it, while in the batch prepared for Le Mans the best produced more than 500bhp (SAE). And by that time, after exposing many failures, the dynamometer tests were proving durability.

Presumably, the cost of engine failures was acceptable, for the helicopter windscreen wiper blades fitted were reckoned to be more expensive than the V8s!

The Kar Kraft transaxle had the same qualities of sturdiness, albeit with a weight penalty, and the bugs were ironed out of it, too. Considerable work was put into the development of two automatic transmissions, both using the torque converter from the production Falcon. Mk IIs were to run with an automatic box in 1966, but it never came up to expectations because of power loss in the torque converter.

The Mk II was a heavy car, with a startline weight of 2,660lb (1,208kg), and there were

In side elevation the J-1 looked distinctly stubby with its high tail contrasting strongly with the low lines of the nose section.

They either liked it or loathed it. Reactions to the J ranged from 'the most handsome car to come out of the whole programme' to 'what looks right is right, and the J did not and was not'!

Left: The narrower cockpit of the J echoed European circuit car practice, which had been ignored by Ford in the earlier cars. The odd but distinctive extensions below the headlamps could be removed.

Right: The rear spoiler, which was added to the J for the 1966 Le Mans test weekend. The roof mirror is clearly visible and the NACA engine air intake can be seen on the centreline of the bodywork.

braking problems which could not be solved by using larger units – there was simply no room. The only answer to wear problems was to make allowance for quick changes, and Holman & Moody contrived quick-change discs (a change could be made in four minutes, which compared with the two minutes required to change pads). It was reckoned that one disc change would be called for in a 24-hour race, although in fact at Le Mans in 1966 the two leading cars required only front disc changes, and two pad changes all round. In use the brakes were heavy.

Work on the Mk II had been to make it raceworthy and to incorporate refinements that were predictably worthwhile for 1966, as the IIB. It was felt that the effort needed to sustain it in the front line beyond that season would be disproportionate, so in September 1965 a parallel programme on an advanced successor was put in hand. This GTP (Grand Touring Prototype) emerged in March 1966 as the J car, the first all-American car in the programme. The J designation was owed to Appendix J of the FIA regulations, but the race version developed from it was the Mk IV – another misleading designation as this car was far removed from a fourth version of the GT40.

The J

The J used the suspension and power unit of the Mk II and had the same wheelbase, but slightly narrower track dimensions. The chassis and body were substantially different, in particular with the hull built up of aircraft-type epoxy-bonded aluminium honeycomb sandwich, with bonded and rivetted mounting

A specimen of the aluminium honeycomb sandwich material which was used in the hull of the J and subsequently in the Mk IV.

points. This was 181lb lighter than a Mk II chassis, with a similar degree of torsional rigidity. Doors, and nose and tail panels, were of reinforced glassfibre.

The monocoque was designed by Ed Hull and built by the Brunswick Corporation, which was familiar with honeycomb sandwich techniques through its work with aircraft components, and was delivered to Kar Kraft, where suspension and engine mounting points were bonded in place with adhesive that was brewed and heated at Dearborn – reproducing that process was to make life difficult for a restorer some 15 years later! The honeycomb sandwich was suspect only in respect of heavy local loadings, and thread inserts were used for reinforcement by conventional means at these points.

Kar Kraft completed the cars, which in overall layout did not depart greatly from the GT40 or Mk II, and fitted the bodywork sections made at the Ford Design Center. Overall, the J was some 400lb lighter than a Mk II, was more compact and had a smaller frontal area (measuring 14.8sq ft compared with 15.8sq ft), and with the same power as the Mk II should in theory have been faster. But tests with the J were disappointing in this respect, suggesting flaws in aerodynamic reasoning. Quite simply, there was an over-reaction to the plethora of aerodynamic

research early in the GT40 programme, which often proved misleading, especially with wind-tunnel findings. So the approach to the J was to package the components, then get the aerodynamics right by trying alternative configurations of body panels and spoilers on a complete car.

Outwardly, the J was perhaps the most distinctive car in the series, especially at the rear, where the roof line was carried through from a narrower cockpit to the tail. A clear-view 'tunnel' was expected to give adequate rear vision, but eventually exterior mirrors had to be tried and a roof-mounted mirror was adopted. The square-cut tail allowed room for the luggage space called for in the international regulations. The J proved to be a much more sensitive car than the Mk II, Bruce McLaren reckoning 'it felt like a racer'. Chris Amon later recalled that he had worried that 'it might come unglued'; out of the box, he rated it no better than a Mk II during the Le Mans tests, but saw its obvious potential (Chris did set the fastest lap of the weekend in J-1).

Although the intention was that J-2 should be run in some late-1966 CanAm races as part of the development programme, the Js turned out to be test vehicles. J-1 saw extensive use, in the 1966 Le Mans tests as well as in more private circuit work and in a wind-tunnel.

Above: Stalwarts of the Ford development and race programmes, Ken Miles, Bruce McLaren and Chris Amon, with J-1 at Le Mans for the April 1966 tests. *Below:* An unusually chubby-faced McLaren seems to have provoked an amused response from Miles as Ken holds an imaginary steering wheel, while Amon seems deep in thought.

The second J at Riverside, being driven by Ken Miles. This lightweight version was intended for possible Group 7 use. Outwardly, the nose was revised, the NACA engine air intake was well forward in the roof and the air intakes behind the doors were lower. The test programme came to an end in tragic circumstances when Miles lost his life in a high-speed accident on the Californian circuit.

Ken Miles, an expatriate Englishman who came to dominate sportscar racing on America's West Coast, and whose great skill as a development driver was to be so beneficial to Ford as they came to grips with a hitherto unfamiliar branch of racing.

J-2 was a lightweight sports-racing variant, and some saw it as a pointer to the route that might be taken in the evolution of the J as an endurance car, as a means by which it might be made competitive. However, it covered very few miles before it was destroyed in the tragic accident at Riverside that cost the life of Ken Miles in August 1966.

Outwardly, the third J had an 'endurance' body on similar lines, but with four headlights and a revised tail. It was used in back-to-back trials with a Mk II, then suffered a major suspension failure during tests at Daytona late in 1966. After more test work early in 1967 it was fitted with a Mk IV body (following J-4, which was completed in this form). At the Le Mans test weekend in 1967, McLaren exceeded 200mph in it down the Mulsanne straight. It was then retired, and the J story picks up as the Mk IV story . . .

Meanwhile, the X-1 was rebuilt by Shelby after its short career as a sports-racing car, in effect as a spyder version of the Mk II, with the nose and tail bodywork of that model, and in that guise it won the second race of 1966.

Ford went into that season with a formidable armoury, and with every sign of using the cars in the steamroller campaign some European teams had feared since the American company entered international racing – Ferrari played this propaganda card for all it was worth!

6

1966 Le Mans

Third time lucky

In 1966, Ford contested the two American early-season races in strength, facing only modest opposition, then left the spring European events to independent teams and the victories – with one startling exception – to Ferrari.

The opening race at Daytona was a full 24-hour event in 1966, and lasting the distance was a greater challenge to the Ford teams than the pair of independent Ferrari 330P2s or the lone Chaparral. Ken Miles was fastest in practice, and although Bonnier was threateningly close in the Chaparral, that car was to lose almost an hour with steering problems early in the race. Fords finished 1-2-3-5, Miles and Ruby winning at 108.02mph, 173.80km/h in Shelby's 1015, with a NART Ferrari hard-driven by Rodriguez and Andretti splitting the procession in fourth place. Only one Mk II retired, the automatic transmission car driven by Ginther and Bucknum, when its transmission failed. The GT40s did not fare so well and none were running at the end, although the Sutcliffe/Grossman car lasted through to the closing minutes (when its engine failed) and was classified as a finisher, thus scoring championship points. The Essex Wire team made its debut under David Yorke, both its GT40s retiring with gearbox failures, although one was credited with 17th place.

At Sebring, the result in 1-2-3 terms was similar, although the test was sterner, as much because of the demands on brakes as the opposition. This included a new works Ferrari 330P3 as well as a pair of Chaparrals. Holman & Moody ran two Mk IIs, Shelby a Mk II and the rebodied X-1, while Alan Mann ran two of his lightweight cars. The Mk II roadster (the erstwhile X-1) practised with automatic transmissions (the plural because of failures), but raced with a standard four-speed manual gearbox. Driven by Miles and Ruby, it was not impressive in practice, but it won the race (at 98.067mph, 157.79km/h), rather fortunately as the leading Gurney/Grant Mk II expired in the closing laps. The bumpy Florida airfield circuit stressed the light-alloy chassis of the X-1 to the limit, and after its victory the car was adjudged beyond repair, although it was not officially scrapped until 1970. The Gurney/Grant car was excluded from the results: it would have been second had Dan Gurney not decided to push it when a scavenge pump failure led to its engine stopping within minutes of the finish. Both of Mann's 4.7-litre cars retired, and while Mk IIs were classified second and 12th, there had been unwelcome signs of unreliability, especially with brakes on the Foyt/Bucknum car. Moreover, when the works Ferrari was running it had challenged for the lead. The GT40 record was better: five were classified and six retired, with Scott and Revson in one of the Essex Wire cars finishing third overall. Unhappily, Canadian Bob McLean was killed when his Comstock GT40 rolled into a telegraph pole and caught fire.

The Le Mans test days came only a week

The Mk II was well developed and raceworthy by 1966. This example, 1013, run by Shelby and driven by Miles and Ruby, won the 24-hour race at Daytona which opened the Championship season.

later, and some cars were flown direct from Florida to France. During that first weekend in April, the J was a centre of attention, coupled with speculation about the absence of Ferrari. Shelby ran Mk IIs, trying one with an automatic transmission, and the J, while Mann had a pair of the 'special' GT40s; standard cars were run by Filipinetti, Ford France and Comstock.

The first day was wet, and most drivers circulated cautiously, well aware that they were testing. However, veteran Walt Hansgen apparently ignored advice to respect the conditions – he lapped within 11 seconds of the record – and was fatally injured in an accident. His Shelby Mk II aquaplaned as he passed the pits and instead of taking the Dunlop curve it went straight on; there was a road ahead, but it was too short to be an escape road, and the car was wrecked against a sand barrier (like several 'wrecked' cars in

the series, this one was later the basis for a reconstruction).

The second day was dry, and Chris Amon lapped faster and faster in the J, despite its load of equipment to record brake temperatures, engine speeds, lift and so on. Before the car expired, he lapped in 3min 34.4sec. In subsequent tests in the USA, however, the J did not match a normal Mk II in speed or reliability, so the possibility that it might be raced began to fade. At Le Mans, Miles lapped a Mk II in 3min 39.3sec, while in one of the Mann cars Jackie Stewart got down to 3min 38.6sec (for the same team, Whitmore recorded 3min 41.2sec and Hawkins 3min 51.3sec). Mairesse and Muller were credited with 3min 44.7sec and 3min 50.7sec in the Filipinetti car, and Greder with 3min 50.9sec for Ford France.

The best of these times seemed to confirm suggestions that the 4.7-litre GT40 had been dismissed prematurely, and the results of spring races in Europe further encouraged this view. In the Monza 1,000km race Whitmore and Gregory placed an Essex Wire car second overall behind a works Ferrari 330P3, while Muller and Mairesse were third in a Filipinetti GT40. Ford France sent Ligier and Greder to the Targa Florio – perhaps the least suitable race for a GT40 – and although the car stopped a few kilometres short of the finish it was credited with 12th place overall and a class victory.

In search of championship points, a rather tired Mk II was run in the Spa 1,000km race by Alan Mann – it was outpaced by Parkes and Scarfiotti in both practice and the race, but nevertheless finished second to the Ferrari. An Essex Wire GT40 was third (driven by Scott and Revson) and Sutcliffe shared his car with Redman to take fourth place. The 1,000km race at the Nürburgring saw Hill and Bonnier give the Chaparral team a victory in their first race in Europe, while the best-placed GT40 was the Ford France car driven by Ligier and Schlesser, fifth.

But that seemed of little account, as the main Ford teams were on the move towards Le Mans. This time there were to be no mistakes: eight Mk IIs were entered, three each by Shelby and Holman & Moody, two by Alan Mann (at one time, Ford had aspired to enter 15 Mk IIs!). It seemed almost incidental that six GT40s were also accepted, albeit one as a reserve; five started in the race, for the reserve entry car was written off in a practice accident. The three main teams were all based in a Peugeot garage.

As a spur, Henry Ford II was the honoured guest of the ACO, and was to start the race. 'Henry Expects You To Win' has an apocryphal ring to it, but the source of the catch phrase was a card circulated in the Dearborn offices before the race . . . this was to be the year when Ford won, and finally got a return for a multi-million dollar investment.

Most top drivers were still prepared to undertake the 24-hour race in the mid-1960s, but even so the official Ford teams had problems in contracting 16 of sufficient calibre – problems that were compounded when Lloyd Ruby was injured in an aircraft accident and A J Foyt and Jackie Stewart in racing

This Mk II (1011) was reduced to scrap in the accident which cost Walt Hansgen his life at Le Mans in April 1966.

The X-1, rebodied as a Mk II roadster, at Sebring in 1966. Ken Miles and Lloyd Ruby drove it to victory in the 12-hour race.

One of the GT40s campaigned by the Essex Wire team in 1966. This car, shared by David Hobbs and Jochen Neerpasch, retired from the 1,000km race at Spa-Francorchamps, but Skip Scott and Peter Revson drove the team's other car into third place.

accidents. The eventual pairings were: Shelby American – McLaren/Amon, Miles/Hulme, Gurney/Grant; Holman & Moody – Donohue/Hawkins, Andretti/Bianchi, Bucknum/Hutcherson; Alan Mann – Graham Hill/Thompson, Whitmore/Gardner.

However, Dick Thompson was involved in the practice accident with the reserve GT40, when it was being driven slowly by American amateur driver Dick Holqvist, who was apparently heedless of his mirrors. In the type of accident that led most top drivers to shun

the event in the following years, Holqvist simply moved over onto the line of the much faster Mk II at White House and the GT40 was punted off the road. On this occasion Thompson was blameless, but he failed to stop and report the accident, and for that misdemeanour the ACO officials decided to exclude his car from the race. They backed down when the Ford brinkmanship response was to threaten to withdraw all of their official entries, and the face-saving outcome was to disqualify Thompson. Mann arranged for

The second of the Mk IIs run by Shelby at the 1966 Le Mans tests was loaned to Alan Mann Racing for the Spa 1,000km race. Although this was run seven weeks after the tests, the car was still geared for Le Mans. Whitmore and Gardner finished second in the Belgian race, accruing championship points for Ford while AMR gained Mk II experience.

Fords dominate the start at Le Mans in 1966. No 3 in the centre is the Gurney/Grant Mk II, and No 1 is the Miles/Hulme car that finished second. The eventual winner (No 2) has not moved, while the Hawkins/Donohue Mk II (No 4) is already pursuing Hill's car.

Mission almost accomplished. The car shared by Bruce McLaren and Chris Amon (1046) splashing past the pits on the way to Ford's historic first victory at Le Mans in 1966. At the third attempt, Ford dominated the race.

Brian Muir to take his place at very short notice, and the ACO allowed him two familiarization laps outside official practice periods. That was little enough for any driver to learn the car and the circuit, and the American contingent was very sceptical about the new recruit, but in the race Muir was to complement Hill admirably, and lap consistently in around 3min 40sec.

That was 10 seconds outside the fastest practice lap of 3min 30.6sec (142.979mph,

230.103km/h) set by Dan Gurney (moreover, Dan had lapped in 3min 33.3sec in the dark during the first session). The Ferrari drivers could not hope to match this pace (and the second-line Ferraris were out-qualified by GT40s), so the Italian team's strategy was to race fast enough to push the Fords, if possible with some revs in hand, and to rely on the greater economy of the P3, in respect of tyres and brakes as well as fuel consumption. Yet the Ferrari team was crumbling almost before

The staged dead-heat that didn't quite come off. Ken Miles and Denny Hulme were officially classified second in a near photo-finish, with the third-placed Bucknum/Hutcherson Mk II in their wake.

practice started, when Nino Vaccarella threatened to walk out when he found that he was to drive a Dino instead of the P3 he expected. Worse, John Surtees could not accept team manager Dragoni's dictats about his role, for these were contrary to his agreement with Ferrari, and he did leave.

Fastest of the Ferraris was an open P3 entered by NART, but generally the Fords were dominant, and there was an air of confidence as the cars were lined up with their tails toward the pit counters early on Saturday afternoon. Since 1965 the order had been determined by practice times, rather than engine capacity, and in 1966 all 13 Fords were in the top 20:

Gurney/Grant (Ford Mk II)	3:30.6
Miles/Hulme (Ford Mk II)	3:31.7
Whitmore/Gardner (Ford Mk II)	3:32.2
McLaren/Amon (Ford Mk II)	3:32.6
Ginther/Rodriguez (Ferrari P3)	3:33.0
G. Hill/Thompson* (Ford Mk II)	3:33.2
Scarfiotti/Parkes (Ferrari P3)	3:34.3
Bandini/Guichet (Ferrari P3)	3:34.4
Bucknum/Hutcherson (Ford Mk II)	3:34.6
Bonnier/P. Hill (Chaparral)	3:35.1
Hawkins/Donohue (Ford Mk II)	3:35.2
Andretti/L. Bianchi (Ford Mk II)	3:36.3
Scott/Revson (Ford GT40)	3:40.2
Neerpasch/Ickx (Ford GT40)	3:43.7
Mairesse/Muller (Ferrari P2)	3:44.6
Bondurant/Gregory (Ferrari P2)	3:45.0
Rindt/Ireland (Ford GT40)	3:45.6
Dumay/'Beurlys' (Ferrari P2)	3:46.3
Sutcliffe/Spoerry (Ford GT40)	3:47.6
Ligier/Grossman (Ford GT40)	3:47.8

*Thompson's place taken by Muir.

For the third time Fords led the opening stages of a Le Mans 24-hour race, and in 1966 their lead was hardly challenged. Graham Hill

Henry Ford II checks the watch of his racing manager Leo Beebe as they await the end of the 1966 Le Mans race. The man whose name is over the shop seems to be the less concerned.

It's all over, the rain has stopped and there's even been time to clean the cars before Bruce McLaren drives slowly back past the crowd opposite the pits, Chris Amon returns their waves and their two mechanics enjoy the ride. The car behind was the Mk II driven into third place by Ronnie Bucknum and Dick Hutcherson.

led the first lap, followed by Gurney, Bucknum, Parkes in the first Ferrari, Whitmore, and Bonnier in the Chaparral. Miles stopped for a door to be closed, restarted and broke the lap record several times (getting down to 3min 31.1sec on his 15th lap, although Gurney was later to set the record at 3min 30.6sec, 142.98mph, 230.05km/h), and he had recovered to fifth at the end of the first hour. Hawkins stopped at the same time with a broken half-shaft (the stop cost him 70 minutes), and Whitmore was delayed with a fractured brake pipe and a clutch problem. There were always enough Fords, although at dusk Ferraris were second and fourth, and there was a feeling that

Sunday morning might just see the Italian cars rolling on reliably towards another Le Mans victory . . .

But however well the Ferrari strategy seemed to be working on Saturday evening, by half-distance the effective Ferraris were out of the race and the first six places were held by Fords. The three Shelby cars, headed by Miles and Hulme, led and were followed by the surviving Holman & Moody Mk II and the Essex Wire and Filipinetti GT40s. The Hawkins/Donohue Mk II had gone out with a broken differential in the first four hours, and so had the Rindt/Ireland GT40 with a blown piston. The four hours to midnight saw the Andretti/Bianchi Ford retire with valve failure, the Hill/Muir car when a suspension upright broke and the Whitmore/Gardner car with clutch failure.

The big Fords were slowed through the daylight hours on Sunday, revs being kept down to around 5,000rpm and lap times to a safe four minutes – the only threat was distant, from the Porsches now many laps behind. Nevertheless, the engines in two more GT40s failed (the 4.7-litre V8 was still not up to the long high-speed run down the Mulsanne straight, lap after lap, hour after hour). Dieter Spoerry crashed in the Esses, spinning on his own car's liquids when a fuel filler cap opened. Before noon, the one-time leading Ford was out, too, coolant exhausted and its engine cooked.

Three Fords remained, cruising. At noon, the McLaren/Amon and Miles/Hulme cars had both completed 303 laps, and the Bucknum/Hutcherson Mk II was nine laps behind in third place. The lead changed with pit stops, and Ford minds turned to the possibility of the first dead heat in the history of the race. McLaren and Miles were duly instructed. Two things spoiled this publicity ploy: Ken Miles slowed slightly in the formation finish, and the ACO ruled that his car had in any case been some 20 metres nearer the actual starting line on Saturday afternoon than McLaren's, therefore McLaren and Amon had covered the greater distance. In the 1990s, there were attempts to change history as a US lobby called for a re-audit of the official lap charts on the basis of Shelby documents which suggested that the first two positions should be reversed!

Ford's third attempt to win the greatest 24-hour race had ended in triumph. McLaren and Amon had driven a controlled race, and had cruised the closing hours, yet had covered 3,003.369 miles, or 4,833.23 kilometres, at an average speed of 125.14mph, 201.385km/h. Dan Gurney had set a new lap record, the Miles/Hulme Mk II was even third equal in the Index of Thermal Efficiency (recording 39.85 litres/100kms, or 7.1mpg)*.

Within the term of the adage that three years were needed to develop a Le Mans winner, Ford had won at a cost estimated in contemporary reports to be $9 million – this by no means to Ford's discredit, for they could challenge priceless experience only with resources. As a bonus, the GT40s won the Production Car Championship, too. Many people in the company thought that one Le Mans victory was enough, and that if gained, and however sweeping, a second victory would not pay remotely similar dividends. Nevertheless, in July, the decision was taken to continue the programme in 1967.

Only minor races, contested by independent entrants, remained in 1966, and the results were mixed. Winter passed without the 1967 car taking shape.

---

*At that time the Index of Thermal Efficiency was more highly rated by the ACO than their time-honoured Index of Performance. Its carefully calculated handicap formula took into account fuel consumption, weight and speed, but not engine size. In 1966, weight and average speed meant that the Ford Mk II had a fuel consumption target of 5.4mpg, and it improved on this by some 31% (3% less than the Efficiency award-winning 1.3-litre Alpine-Renault).

7

Diverging Paths

Mk IV and the Mirage

The development programme for the new season was severely set back by Miles' Riverside accident; it was impossible to pinpoint a mechanical or structural failure as the cause – aerodynamic lift was thought to be the probable reason – but confidence in the J as such drained away. One result was that the definitive 1967 car did not start to take shape until the spring of that year. By that time, Leo Beebe had moved on, and had been succeeded by Jacque Passino, with John Cowley continuing in his role. Control of the two retained teams (Shelby and Holman & Moody) was to become more centralized, although no head office edicts could persuade them to become the best of friends . . .

At the end of 1966, Ford Advanced Vehicles was formally wound up, too. This was a tiny operation by Ford standards, and although there was talk of absorbing it into Ford of Britain, nothing came of this. However, John Wyer and John Willment were encouraged to set up JW Automotive Engineering, to take over the Slough plant on favourable terms – indeed, with a modest Ford subsidy to continue the manufacture of GT40s, maintain a parts and service operation, and provide support services for private entrants. Apart from ensuring continuity, this showed that although FAV had almost been cold-shouldered out of the mainstream racing activities, John Wyer's efforts had not gone unappreciated in Dearborn. It was also to lead to valuable racing successes in the name of

Ford which could hardly have been foreseen late in 1966 . . .

By 1967, Wyer was able to run a racing programme on the lines he had envisaged for the GT40 – he had long held that the original design could have been developed in conventional simple ways, and now he was able to do it his way, and with his own men. He had, of course, been privy to the earlier stillborn 'lightweight' project by Ford of Britain, seeing it as a wasted opportunity and the way to move forward, and now he had the backing of the Gulf Oil Corporation to put his case to the test. Gulf's involvement came about at the instigation of their Executive Vice-President, Grady Davis, a racing enthusiast with whom Wyer had enjoyed a growing relationship in 1966. By the end of that year a Gulf racing venture had been agreed, with the not unusual claim that it was an extension of normal product development, but highly unusual for a fuel company in that Gulf did not simply sponsor it, but underwrote the whole racing programme and actually owned the cars. It was to be a very fruitful partnership, for both Gulf and JW Automotive, while Ford enjoyed some well-deserved 'rub-off' benefits.

GT40s were to race with distinction in the light blue and orange Gulf colours, but in 1967 the effort centred on a derivative, which was ready in the spring and given the name Mirage, apparently as Davis was unhappy that Ford would not actively assist in the project.

Two views of an early J under construction at Kar Kraft. The elegantly curved side boxes linked with the front and rear transverse bulkheads to form a substantial and rigid structure. In the definitive Mk IV the curve gave way to squared angular lines.

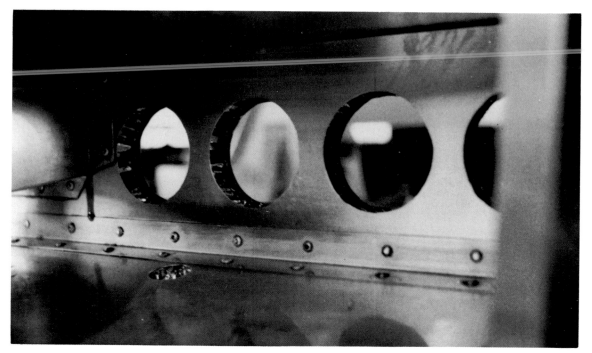

These holes in the front bulkhead indicate the thickness of the honeycomb sandwich material used in the construction of the Mk IV chassis structure.

The name was almost universally acceptable; Ford did not object, until the Mirage started scoring championship points, when it was realized that those points would not be credited to Ford . . .

Despite JW Automotive commitments to parallel work on production GT40s, as well as to a handful of the less spartan Mk III road versions for its introduction in April 1967, work on the first Mirage M1 moved ahead smoothly, if hurriedly.

In America, on the other hand, there had been a natural pause to draw breath, and then the period of indecision following Miles' accident. In the autumn of 1966, the 1967 policy had been defined: both the Mk II and the J were to be developed. Late in the year, back-to-back tests were run, which showed that progress had been made in overcoming persistent shortcomings in the brakes, but that there were considerable aerodynamic problems with the J – in later Daytona tests it failed to match Mk II speeds. Moreover, neither car could equal Ferrari's test times – in a nicely calculated move, the Italians, backed by Firestone, had thrown down the gauntlet by running a full series of tests with the

prototype of the new 330P4 at Daytona. It completed 580 laps, and achieved a rumoured 210mph, although on the Mulsanne straight at Le Mans P4s failed to reach 195mph. So for the Daytona race the two Ford teams ran six Mk IIs, three rebuilt 1966 cars and three new. All were marginally heavier, for a weight-saving exercise had been more than offset by the addition of full rollcages and built-in fire extinguisher systems. There was no immediate compensation for a change in weight distribution as the oil tank had been moved from front to back.

The 427 engines had dual carburettors, and there was a reversion to cast-iron heads, with larger valves. Any increase in car weight was to be accompanied by a more than proportional increase in power, with up to 530bhp (around 500bhp was the Le Mans target) to be put on the road through a strengthened transmission. There were to be further slight revisions to the Mk IIB before Le Mans, but the immediate problem was its successor. In a crash programme at Kar Kraft, a new glassfibre body for the J was designed, built, wind-tunnel tested and then track-tested within a month. In this guise it was to become

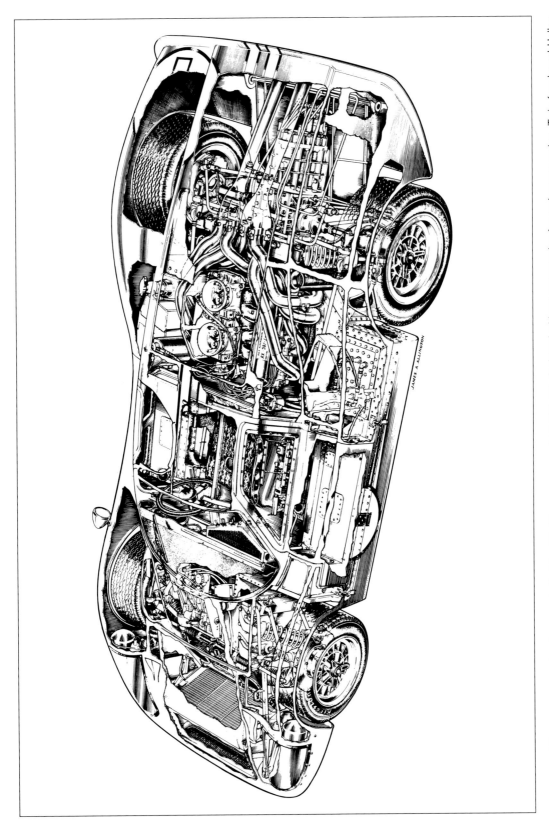

This James Allington cutaway drawing reveals that the Mk IV was a very substantial car, designed without compromise for endurance racing. Twin four-barrel Holley carburettors nestled between the cylinder banks of the 427 engine and large-diameter exhaust pipes threaded their way over the T-44 transmission. Quick-action switchgear was mounted on a panel to the left of the steering wheel and the passenger's space was occupied by inert-gas fire extinguisher equipment.

the Mk IV. It appeared more handsome and functional than the Mk II, and it worked – drag was substantially lower and it was a little lighter; these qualities showed in back-to-back tests in March, when the Mk IV was markedly faster than a Mk IIB.

Externally, the nose derived from the third J, while the tail was swept down to a full-width adjustable spoiler (atop a pronounced overhang), which enabled a conventional rear window to be used. The oil cooler intakes which had been low on the flanks of the Group 7 car were immediately behind the doors on the Mk IV, with the door surface in the flanks immediately below the windows recessed to feed air to the intakes. Engine air was taken in through flush inlets immediately behind the cockpit at driver-head level (external scoops were found to produce a considerable increase in drag), while NACA ducts fed air to the rear brakes. Air inlets at the nose varied, with only the first cars having separate brake air inlets, while one or two NACA ducts were used for cockpit air. Rear fins were to be tried, and discarded. After the

tests, the lower edges of the sills were squared-off in a move towards controlling the airflow under the car.

At angle joints in the epoxy resin-bonded aluminium honeybomb chassis, external and internal metal strips, triple-rivetted, were added as precautionary strengthening as it was realized that a car would be routinely subject to shock loadings seldom encountered with an aircraft. It was claimed that this structure was 88 per cent lighter than a conventional steel chassis of comparable stiffness, although, of course, the steel yardstick was of value only in Ford terms and not applicable to the wider world of competition cars.

The car in its original form weighed around 2,380lb (1,080kg) dry, compared with the Mk II's 2,700lb (1,226kg), but by the time the teams got to Le Mans weight had risen to around 2,600lb; the Ferrari 330P4 weighed 1,960lb (890kg) and the spectacular winged Chaparral 2F was slightly lighter at 1,941lb (881kg). A substantial rollcage was incorporated, and in the one major race accident involving a Mk IV the chassis stood

There was also need for some less sophisticated work during the Le Mans tests. A pair of tin snips was put to work to slim down the tail spoiler before stabilizing fins were added to J-3.

up well to a heavy impact, for although it was distorted 'beyond repair', that assessment reflected the fine limits to which it had been built and the impracticality of rejigging such a structure, although it was to be revised in the 1980s when it seemed that any wrecked car of value could be rebuilt.

In common with the Mk IIB, 15in and 16in wheels were to be used, with 12in ventilated disc brakes (the 'turbo' wheels were intended to draw air across the brakes). The accidents to Hansgen and Miles had made Ford extremely safety-conscious, and as a contribution to that end inner tyre liners were used, despite the penalty of increased weight.

The fifth J was the first car to be built from scratch as a Mk IV, and so designated. However, J-4 was converted to this specification and shape, and its successful race

debut at Sebring led to the decision to run four Mk IVs at Le Mans. J-3 was also converted, and was sent to the Le Mans test weekend, where Ford encountered the first Mirage M1.

Len Bailey had taken the GT40 as the basis for this car; the chassis was slightly modified, while the body was lighter and smoother, with a pronounced tumblehome above the waistline and a finer nose.

A narrower cockpit was allowed by the regulations, and had been postulated for the stillborn lightweight GT40 project initiated by Ford of Britain. Coupled with a revised nose, the reduced frontal area and more slippery shape gave a modest drag figure improvement (a Cd of 0.33 compared with 0.35). A Mk II single radiator outlet was used above the nose, while an adjustable tail spoiler was tried.

At first a 4.7-litre engine was used (an

By 1966, production GT40s were familiar cars at most levels of racing, and in other forms of competition. This is a fairly late car (1072) blasting through the farmyard on the Harewood hillclimb in the hands of its first owner, John Cussins, early in 1968.

The Mirage made its public debut at the 1967 Le Mans trials. This is M0001, driven by Attwood, which survives by the happy accident that it was out of the country when its sister M10003 was rebuilt as a GT40 (the third Mirage was destroyed in an accident).

improved version in that some special parts became available) while a 5-litre V8 was installed for the M1's first race. JWA hoped to eliminate the lingering head gasket weakness through the use of Cooper gaskets. A full Holman & Moody 5.7-litre engine was used in the car which scored the first Mirage victory, and continued to be used alongside 'normal' 5-litre units and a Gurney 5-litre engine with Gurney-Weslake cylinder heads. Drive was through the customary ZF five-speed gearbox, proven in the GT40, and particular care was taken to ensure adequate brake cooling.

The Gulf team had strength in management, with John Horsman and David Yorke effectively working in harness, the former being the manager away from the circuits and David Yorke the racing manager. The redoubtable Ermanno Cuoghi was chief mechanic, and in Jacky Ickx the team had an outstanding lead driver.

Le Mans remained the principal objective for Ford, while Gulf looked to a full championship season for the Mirages, and of course there were independent GT40s run by teams with widely varying capabilities in the field, although it seemed that the day of the GT40 in mainline events had passed

8

Season of Success

The 1967 climax

Ford had a record to defend in 1967, and could not ignore the two early-season American races. Their two teams each entered three Mk IIs for the Daytona event in February, one of each trio running as a 'Mercury', and neither team had an easy time. Apart from handling problems in practice, there was the spectre of those very successful Ferrari trials and the sight of the Ferrari team relaxed and confident before the actual race. For most of practice, Ferrari was in contest with Chaparral for the leading grid places, until in the final session Gurney did manage to take pole for Ford, achieving his time of 1min 55.1sec with the aid of tyres which would have been described as 'qualifiers' a few years on, and an excess of engine revs. The winged 7-litre Chaparral 2F and three Ferraris were next on the time sheets, then the Andretti/Ginther Mk II.

The race turned out to be a disaster for Ford as improperly heat-treated output shafts in the gearboxes failed in rapid succession, until the spares available were used. The two best-placed cars got replacements from an older batch, hastily cannibalized from test cars, and one of these Mk IIs lasted the race, finishing seventh despite a failing head gasket.

Three Ferraris finished in formation, 1-2-3, returning Ford's gesture at the end of the 1966 Le Mans race, and that did not fail to make an impression in Dearborn. Ford rushed the Mk IV through for the next race, and sensibly made no attempt to use it as a demonstration, but rather as a serious race test (in that respect the Sebring event lacked the important element of front-line Ferraris).

The Gulf team had made a token entry at Daytona, using Grady Davis' personal GT40. At the end of the race it was the highest-placed Ford – sixth being far and away the best placing so far for a GT40 in a 24-hour race – and as it had lost almost an hour with an electrical problem this performance was hardly balm for Dearborn . . .

The showing at Sebring just had to be better – a victory would prove little, as the opposition was weak, and the objective was to prove the Mk IV. Tests at Daytona had been encouraging, for Andretti had lapped in times below Gurney's pole-position time for the 24-hour race, and at Sebring, McLaren was fastest in practice in the new car, in 2min 48.0sec. That was 2.6sec faster than the Chaparral 2F and 5.6sec faster than the other 'official' Ford in the race, a Mk II being run for comparison (this had a revised tail with the spare wheel stowed vertically to the left of the gearbox, and improved ducting in the nose, anticipating the Mk IIB).

Once the Chaparrals had fallen out, the two Fords led the race unchallenged. McLaren and Andretti won in the Mk IV at 103.13mph, 165.94km/h, while the Mk II sat at its pit with a broken camshaft for the last half-hour, yet was still classified second overall! Apart from an opening duel between McLaren and Mike Spence, in the Chaparral 2F, it had been a dull

The highest-placed Ford in the 1967 Daytona 24-hour race was Grady Davis' production GT40 (1049), seen here at a night pit stop, which was run by the infant JWA team and driven into sixth place by Ickx and Thompson.

An oddity of the 1967 Daytona race was a pair of Mk IIs entered as 'Mercury GTs', one of which is being challenged here by a Chaparral early in the race. Drivers of this car were Gurney and Foyt.

The best result by a works Ford at Daytona was achieved with this Shelby Mk II, which was nursed through to seventh place by Bruce McLaren (seen driving here while being pursued by the winning Ferrari) and Lucien Bianchi.

race, but the performance of the Mk IV encouraged Ford to push ahead with it.

The next commitment was to the Le Mans test weekend, where Ford shrewdly ran only two cars, a Mk II and a Mk IV, apparently with more concern for recording data than setting fast times. The cars were fitted with multi-channel recorders, measuring disc temperatures, intake manifold efficiency (findings here led to a modification) and other functions – there were even strain gauges on the drive-shafts. The Mk IV was briefly run with small rear fins in search of a solution to a high-speed instability problem (actually found when the new 16in wheels were discarded in favour of the 15in wheels used previously). Both Goodyear and Firestone tyres were used.

The Fords recorded the fastest official speeds on the Mulsanne straight (Mk IV, 205.05mph, 329.92km/h; Mk II 203.19mph, 326.93km/h), but tended to stop at the pits whenever a fast lap was in prospect. Consequently, the fastest lap times were set by two Ferrari drivers, Bandini and Parkes,

followed by John Surtees in the new Lola-Aston Martin T70 Mk 3. This car was fastest during the second wet day, when Shelby hinted that Ford might have 'gone for a time', but as it was, their best times (the Mk II in 3min 32.6sec, driven by Donohue, and the Mk IV in 3min 36.1sec, driven by McLaren) were well adrift of Bandini's 3min 25.5sec.

The Mirage M1 had run its first tests three weeks earlier, and a second car had been completed for the Le Mans weekend. Both ran with 4.7-litre engines. The first was damaged early in the weekend when David Piper ran out of road in it, while Attwood was sixth fastest in the newer car, in 3min 38.2sec. Neither of the two GT40s present broke 3min 50sec.

The Ford contingent returned to America to run another series of dynamometer tests – similar to those run in 1966, but programmed for slightly faster lap speeds and higher engine rpm limits – while JW Automotive had little time to prepare for the 'lesser' races in the European Championship season. Sensibly, the

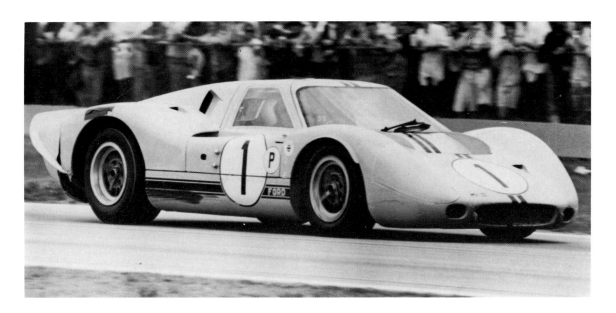

In April 1967, the Sebring race brought a welcome change of fortune for Ford when McLaren and Andretti drove this yellow Mk IV (J-4) to an encouraging victory in its first race.

J-3 at the 1967 Le Mans test weekend, running with small rear fins that were subsequently to be discarded. The driver is McLaren.

A GT40 (1003) in Ford France colours, near Collesano during the 1967 Targa Florio, when it was placed fifth. In 1966 it was fitted with a standard nose and was one of the first GT40s to race in this form. In a 10-race life with the Ford France team (although the car was owned by Ligier and Giorgi) it failed to finish only once.

Mirages were not taken to the Targa Florio, although oddly, of the four events run in the late spring, the best result for a GT40 was gained in the Sicilian race, when Greder and Giorgi finished fifth in the second car of the Ford France team (the other retired, scenery-damaged).

Before that, the Mirage had made its race debut, and had also gained its first victory. The first race was at Monza, where two cars were run with 5-litre engines. One retired with ignition failure, and the other was delayed by long pit stops to fix an exhaust and mend a shock absorber, Piper and Thompson eventually placing it ninth. Schlesser and Ligier were sixth in a Ford France GT40 (and first in Group 4); Nelson's GT40 was 11th, while among GT40s which retired, the Filipinetti car was destroyed in a fire (that wreck was sold as the basis for a rebuild).

A week later, the 1,000km race at Spa was run in wet conditions. The JWA team had a barely-completed Mirage with a Holman & Moody 5.7-litre engine, and as much to the point they had Jacky Ickx on his home circuit,

and he was second-fastest to Phil Hill (Chaparral) in practice. Ickx led from the start, while Piper crashed the second Mirage on the eighth lap. In a clever tactical move, David Yorke left Ickx in the car after the first refuelling stop and then used Dick Thompson to relieve him (Thompson had been nominated for the second car). The Mirage won by a lap, at 120.49mph, 193.90km/h, and once again GT40s headed the large-engine Group 4 category, Sutcliffe and Redman finishing sixth and Salmon and Oliver taking eighth, while two other GT40s retired with engine failures.

Few teams made the long trip to Sicily, and Ferrari did not send the front-line P4s to the third 1,000km race, at the Nürburgring. In practice, Dick Thompson crashed the Mirage with the Gurney-Weslake engine, so the team started only Ickx and Attwood, in a car with a Holman & Moody 5.7-litre V8. Once the lone Chaparral and the Lola-Aston Martin had fallen out early in the race, that Mirage was the only car to challenge a mass of Porsches. It ran as high as second before stopping on the

Jacky Ickx waiting to take a spell at the wheel of a JWA Mirage (M10003) during practice for the 1,000km race at Spa-Francorchamps, which was to bring the team its first victory.

Ickx, as ever, was in his element when the conditions at Spa made the track treacherous. The pronounced tumblehome of the cockpit sides compared with the GT40 is most noticeable from this angle.

circuit with two flat tyres. Three GT40s finished in the top 10, Greder and Giorgio taking seventh place and a class win, by half a minute from Crabbe and Pierpoint.

There were just 10 days between the German race and first practice at Le Mans – justification enough for Ferrari to ignore the ADAC 1,000kms, while teams such as Mirage had little time to prepare for the 24-hour race. The Ford teams' preparations had, of course, been uninterrupted since the test weekend, and for the first meeting with Ferrari since the Daytona debacle they lined up a formidable heavy brigade of 7-litre cars. Shelby and Holman & Moody each entered two Mk IVs and a Mk IIB, while a Holman & Moody Mk IIB was entered by Ford France. Each was painted in distinctive individual colours; the Shelby cars ran on Goodyear tyres and the Holman cars on Firestones. A modification was called for by the ACO scrutineers, who quite reasonably decided that an interior rear-view mirror was inadequate (through a sloped window and around the massive carburettors vision was minimal) so external wing mirrors were added. Although the regulations called for a passenger seat which could be occupied, there was no objection to the inert-gas firefighting equipment which filled much of that space.

The two Mirages started practice with 5.7-litre engines; one failed early in practice, so as a precaution both were fitted with 5-litre V8s. Either way, they were outpaced by the 7-litre cars in practice, as were the three GT40s – the Redman/Salmon car belonging to Lord Downe, but run under the wing of JWA, a Ford France car and a Brescia car on loan to Filipinetti. After practice, five of the six fastest cars were Fords, with the Chaparral cast in the role of hare second-fastest overall. The Ford teams suffered minor practice irritants, and a threateningly serious problem with hairline cracks developing in the big windscreens of the Mk IVs, one even when the car was stationary. Incorrect tempering meant that the glass was brittle, but this did not lead to a panic approaching those of the 1965 crises. Corning rushed through a new batch, which was flown across the Atlantic before the race – in first-class seats, as it was felt that unpressurized freight travel could be risky!

Some of the USAC drivers had acclimatization problems, while Gurney and Foyt got at such cross purposes in setting up their car that they sought out McLaren to try it, then asked for it to be put on the settings Bruce had for his race car.

Chaparral had set the pace early in practice,

The Mirages underwent minor alterations prior to the Le Mans race, including the change to larger spotlamps beneath the headlamps. This is the car shared by David Piper and Dick Thompson, which retired with engine trouble during the fifth hour.

but then in the dark of the final session McLaren lapped in 3min 24.7sec (147.316mph, 237.03km/h) – well below the record, and below the best time at the April test days. Nine cars were below the best 1966 qualifying time, six of them Fords. Chaparral had pace, but the stamina of their transmission was suspect. Ferrari did not even have the pace of the test days, and were not sandbagging – if it was wet the skill of their drivers would pay dividends, otherwise Ferrari hopes had to rest on the big American cars failing to last the 24 hours. Ford opinions were that, excluding pit stops, their cars would run the race at a 3min 30sec lap average; Ferrari aimed for 3min 35sec. The disparity in the top 20 times underlined one of the perpetual Le Mans problems, while the extremes were almost absurd: the best lap achieved by the slowest qualifier, a Hrubon, was 5min 08.2sec. The top 20 included all but one of the Fords (the Ford France GT40 was 23rd):

McLaren/Donohue (Ford Mk IV)	3:24.4
Hill/Spence (Chaparral 2F)	3:24.7
Andretti/Bianchi (Ford Mk IV)	3:25.3
Hulme/Ruby (Ford Mk IV)	3:25.5
Hawkins/Bucknum (Ford Mk II)	3:25.8
Gardner/McCluskey (Ford Mk II)	3:26.4
Parkes/Scarfiotti (Ferrari P4)	3:28.9
Rodriguez/Baghetti (Ferrari P4)	3:29.4
Gurney/Foyt (Ford Mk IV)	3:29.8
Mairesse/'Beurlys' (Ferrari P4)	3:30.9
Klass/Sutcliffe (Ferrari P4)	3:33.5
Amon/Vaccarella (Ferrari P4)	3:33.6
Surtees/Hobbs (Lola Mk 3)	3:33.7
Schlesser/Ligier (Ford Mk II)	3:36.1
Ickx/Muir (Mirage)	3:36.3
Piper/Thompson (Mirage)	3:37.0
Attwood/Courage (Ferrari P3)	3:37.8
Salmon/Redman (Ford GT40)	3:38.7
Guichet/Muller (Ferrari P3)	3:39.1
Casoni/Maglioli (Ford GT40)	3:40.8

Ford optimism was borne out in the race, although attrition meant that there was no question of a formation finish at Le Mans in 1967. The Chaparrals lasted longer than many cynics had expected, Phil Hill and Mike Spence in the Texan lead car for a time forcing the Fords to run at a higher pace than the two teams would have wished – the average at four hours was 140.22mph. By that time both Lolas were out, and so was one GT40 after Mike

The field getting away at Le Mans in 1967. Gurney has made a brisk start in the Mk IV (No 1) that he drove to victory, supported by A J Foyt. To its left, Ickx has made up a lot of ground from a lower start position in the Mirage M10003 (No 15), while the McLaren/Donohue Mk IV (No 2) is only just moving. The head-on shot (*below*) gives a powerful impression of the field in one of Le Mans' golden periods.

As the field thundered down to the Esses for the first time in the 1967 Le Mans race, Paul Hawkins led in a Shelby Mk IIB (1047), from Rodriguez's Ferrari, while Ickx's Mirage was ahead of Gurney and two more Fords.

A terrifying sight as Mike Salmon heads towards the sandbank on the outside of Mulsanne corner. Lord Downe's GT40 had burst into flames at high speed after fuel had leaked from a filler cap. The car's right front tyre is already almost off the wheel rim. Salmon managed to roll out of the cockpit before he was too seriously hurt. This car (1026) was slowly rebuilt through the next ten years.

Salmon had brought his spectacularly blazing car to a halt in a sandbank at Mulsanne (spilt fuel had ignited and Salmon was fortunate to escape with burns). The Mirages had retired early, one with valve failure, one with a blown head gasket, leaving the team to wonder whether the 5.7-litre engines should have been used after all. Meanwhile, the Ferrari team seemed to be playing a waiting game to perfection.

The Shelby Fords had run strongly through the opening phase, while the Holman cars ran into minor troubles – a sticking throttle for Denny Hulme (who resumed, to cut the lap record to 3min 23.6sec), lost balance weights for Frank Gardner, a stone-damaged screen for Lucien Bianchi. Through the dusk period, Gurney and Foyt extended their lead in the red Shelby car so that by late Saturday evening it had reached the proportions of laps, and

they still lapped at around 3min 30sec when they might have been expected to ease their pace and consolidate. Gurney's professionalism was taken for granted by knowledgeable Europeans; but Foyt matched it, in an environment still strange to him, and that came as a surprise to many spectators. Lloyd Ruby, on the other hand, was less precise, and the second of his visits to a sandbank ended the race for the car he shared with Hulme.

After 11 hours, Fords comfortably held the first three places; an hour later one of the cars led by five laps, but the next-best was fighting back to sixth place and a third seemed to be out of the running. Ferraris were running reliably in second and fourth places, while the Hill/Spence Chaparral was third, and was to hold that position for another hour. Less than 30 minutes before half-distance three Fords had been eliminated in a multiple incident.

85

A J Foyt prepares to relieve Dan Gurney during their victorious Le Mans race. Just ahead of him, but behind the pit wall, is Homer Perry, while Phil Remington is standing, hands in pockets, alongside the large toolbox. External mirrors were fitted for this race.

Part of the cost of victory at Le Mans. Two of the Fords eliminated early on Sunday morning were Mario Andretti's Mk IV (No 3) and Roger McCluskey's Mk IIB.

Seconds after Andretti and McCluskey had crashed, Jo Schlesser arrived in a Holman & Moody Mk IIB, aimed for a gap between the two wrecks, but hit the bank . . .

The McLaren/Donohue Mk IV entering the Esses after passing Schlesser's wrecked Mk IIB. The tyre marks on the track tell their own story.

The yellow Shelby Mk IV which McLaren and Donohue placed fourth at Le Mans in 1967. *Above:* Donohue prepares to take over from the New Zealander at a pit stop, the car showing signs of hard racing. *Below:* On the Sunday morning this car lost its tail bodywork on the Mulsanne straight; McLaren retrieved it, and it was rebuilt and re-attached to J5 with abundant grey tape. The car ran through to the finish in this condition.

The winning Ford, clean and shining early in the 1967 Le Mans 24-hour race. This view shows off its clean stern lines compared with those of the Mk II.

Andretti had just restarted the bronze Holman & Moody Mk IV after a pit stop when its brake pads had been changed, and as he entered the Esses, a few hundred metres on, a front brake grabbed, turning the car into the banking. It bounced off and came to rest in the road, its nose wrecked. Mario climbed out, collapsed on the banking, and was then taken to Ford's elaborate medical unit, where it was found that he had three broken ribs. He reckoned that the beryllium discs were cracked when Bianchi brought the car in, and that during the pit stop the front pads were put in backwards; some Ford people said that he was told to pump the brakes hard before the Esses, but that they saw no brake lights as J-7 entered the first right-hander . . .

Two cars passed the wreck, but Roger McCluskey, running ninth in the gold Holman Mk II, spun to avoid the Andretti car and hit the bank. Schlesser, in the white Ford France Mk II, aimed for the gap between the two damaged Fords, and also hit the bank. McCluskey got his car back to the pits, where it was found to be too badly damaged to continue. At the same time, the yellow Shelby Mk IV driven by McLaren and Donohue was losing ground as a clutch slave cylinder was replaced, and was to restart 10 laps behind the Mk IV in the lead. The only other survivor was the blue Shelby Mk II driven by Hawkins and Bucknum, which had led the race in the early stages, but had then run into a cooling system problem, which called for welding and dropped it to 42nd place early in the evening.

While the leading car had so many laps in hand that it could be slowed to a careful pace, the Ford back-up was thin. One response was to order Hawkins and Bucknum to run hard, with the aim of getting another car up with the leaders. The drivers responded, climbing back to sixth place by the 16th hour, but little more than an hour later the engine expired, its sump empty. Within the next hour the McLaren/Donohue car shed its engine cover at speed on the straight. McLaren collected it next time round, and at the pits it was crudely repaired with tape and pop rivets, and that cost more time.

The leading Ford cruised serenely through

89

Sunday morning and into the afternoon, with lap times around 3min 45sec; the second-placed Ferrari was lapping at some 10sec a lap faster, although in the remaining hours its team could not hope that a deficit measured in hours could be made up. With an hour to go, the Ferrari team effectively conceded the race, slowing this car to a safe finishing speed.

A J Foyt drove the final stint in the leading Ford, to take the flag. The winning Mk IV had covered 3,251.16 miles, 5,232.00 kilometres, averaging 135.49mph, 218.038km/h, and had even won the Index of Thermal Efficiency (returning 6.5mpg). Hulme and Andretti had become joint lap record-holders, in 3min 23.6sec (147.90mph, 238.014km/h) – in 1963, the year before Ford first went to Le Mans, the record had been set at 3min 53.3sec, 129.07mph, 207.67km/h . . .

Henry Ford II was at Le Mans to join in the celebrations of this all-American victory, which was to be the culmination of his company's efforts in international endurance racing. The decision to rest on laurels had already been taken and more than a decade was to pass before another 'official' Ford – a European Ford – next appeared in the 24-hour race. All save one of the 7-litre coupes were retired, as Ford looked inward to American racing, while at the highest international level the company's name was to be most creditably represented by a Formula 1 engine commissioned by Ford of Britain.

Meanwhile, although it could never be less than the high point of the sportscar season, the Le Mans race did not mark the end of the Championship in 1967, for the BOAC Six Hours at Brands Hatch had been added to the calendar. Before that, the Reims 12-hour race attracted a good entry, including a Holman Mk IIB loaned to Ford France and five GT40s. Two Lolas were fastest in practice, and led through the opening phase, but by two-thirds distance the big Ford was on its own and Schlesser and Ligier drove on to a most comfortable victory, at 127.29mph, 204,81km/h, finishing more than 30 miles ahead of the private Ferrari P2 in second

Champagne time for the winners. From the left, Lodovico Scarfiotti and Mike Parkes join in the celebrations with Dan Gurney and A J Foyt, but Gurney is in charge of the Moet et Chandon!

place. Three of the GT40s finished, but the other two retired.

Championship points ensured that the Brands Hatch race had a much better front-line entry. Flattering to deceive once again, the Lolas were fast in practice, but did not feature on the results sheets. Mike Spence qualified the lone Chaparral 2F third-fastest, and at the end of a frustrating European season for this team their car ran faultlessly as Hill and Spence drove it to a popular victory. Ferrari's second place ensured that the Italian team snatched the Championship from Porsche (co-drivers of the second-placed 330P4 and the third-placed 910 were erstwhile Ford stalwarts Amon and McLaren). Three GT40s were classified in lowly places, and the lone Mirage retired when its second driver, Dick Thompson, crashed. However, the first stint in this car had been driven by Pedro Rodriguez, at the start of his association with JWA, and at two hours he had led the race.

The Montlhéry 1,000kms in the autumn also attracted entries from Mirage and the Ford France Mk IIB. Jacky Ickx' partner in the blue and orange car was Paul Hawkins, who had won six well-supported secondary races in his GT40 in 1967 and had driven a Mirage in one of the minor Swedish races the team contested, to fly the Gulf flag. The French race was run in wet conditions, and the Mirage was headed only briefly, eventually winning by over a lap. The Mk IIB was in a humble fourth

place, and none of the three GT40s which started lasted the distance. At the end of the year, JWA sent the first Mirage to Kyalami for the Rand Nine Hours, getting more race use out of it before it was effectively outlawed from main-line racing (technically, the change of regulations did not come into force for another two months, but there were no more suitable races). Ickx had a new partner, Brian Redman, who was to become another stalwart of endurance racing. They duly won – by 13 laps – and Mirage's season ended on a high note.

Group 7

Ford's first venture into no-holds-barred sportscar racing with the X-1 late in 1965 was low-key and hardly successful, for this one-off, built up at the McLaren factory, was run in four races, but finished only one, when Chris Amon drove it into fifth place in a Riverside race in the Fall professional series (forerunner of CanAm). This car was then rebuilt by Kar Kraft, to all intents and purposes as an open Mk II, and Miles and Ruby drove it to win the 1966 Sebring 12 Hours. It was then set aside, and eventually broken up (a spare chassis apparently survived).

In 1967, Ford started to flirt with CanAm racing, with a sports-racing derivative of the Mk IV, the G7-A. This was undertaken by Kar Kraft, which held four of the honeycomb chassis (a second was to be used in the G7-A

91

The Piper/Thompson Mirage in full flight at Le Mans in 1967. This side elevation shot emphasizes the car's smooth lines.

built up by the Agapiou brothers of Los Angeles, the other two were to be the basis of Mk IVs built in England in the 1980s, albeit one was little more than a floorpan and bulkhead).

The G7-A was open, with neat but hardly sleek glassfibre bodywork, and increased fuel capacity as the cells were extended to the rear of the side boxes. The running gear from the Mk IV was retained – these cars ran notably 'flat', and that was important with the reduced ground clearance of the G7-A. Several engines were used, including a new lightweight aluminium three-valve V8 under development for a 1968 programme that never took shape (a year later it was nevertheless the ephemeral basis for a 25-off Mirage idea), a 7.8-litre (477cu in) unit and a newer 7-litre (429cu in) V8.

The transmission tried on the J and a Ford-engined Lola was brought out again, while a lighter semi-automatic transmission was also developed and fitted to the G7-A for trials. This meant that a driver-controlled rear aerofoil could be tried. It was mounted to the rear suspension, and the wide-chord wing was split at its centre, each half being at a considerable dihedral. It was necesarily supported at mid-span, and the single central strut carried the hydraulic controls. However, the car was usually run without wings, or with a large conventional rear aerofoil. The car was probably too heavy to compete successfully

against the purpose-built cars in the CanAm series, and after track tests Ford quietly gave up the idea of competing in this field.

The test car and the second incomplete car were later handed over to the Agapiou brothers, who completed the second car (J-10) and ran it in some 1969 CanAm races – it turned up for six events, but actually started just three times. It was dogged by engine problems, and made its first start at Edmonton in July, when John Cannon completed five laps in it. Later it was driven – no more successfully – by George Follmer and Jack Brabham. At least the engine did not let the Australian down. A wheel came off . . .

After the 1969 CanAm series, John Cannon drove this G7-A to second place in a non-title race at Mount Fuji, in Japan. He usually drove it in 1970, when it started in six CanAm races, but failed to record a single finish.

The G7-A came as a sad postscript to the Mk IV racing story, and in hindsight it seems extraordinary that Ford allowed it to drag on in independent hands once the basic car was seen to be far from competitive, overweight, under-developed and with suspect engines . . .

Other fields

Ford also made strenuous efforts to provide competitive engines for other CanAm entrants during 1968 and 1969, but otherwise reverted to the pre-GT40 and Indianapolis policy of concentrating on stock and drag racing. Then

The G7-A derivative of the Mk IV nearing completion, with Roy Lunn standing beside the cockpit, and in the centre picture, the car set up for tests in the Dearborn wind-tunnel with an experimental split rear wing. The length of the central strut was variable to allow changes in dihedral, while the angle of incidence was driver-controlled with the left pedal.

The G7-A made little impact on the 1969 CanAm series, when it was usually run without the high wings that had been the subject of so much theoretical and test work. This is John Cannon at Edmonton, Alberta, where he retired with injection problems.

The G7-A again, this time with Jack Brabham at the wheel on the Michigan Speedway, when the car was equipped with a 'barn door' conventional wing on appropriately substantial struts. The Australian retired when a wheel came off.

motorsport was abandoned to Ford's European companies for a while. There was the quite extraordinary record of success for the Ford-Cosworth DFV Formula 1 engine from 1967 – through two decades it powered 154 World Championship race winners, while the DFY variant added another – and derivatives included the equally successful turbocharged DFX for USAC/CART racing, the F1 DFZ and DFR, plus the DFL for endurance racing, while Ford of Britain ran an immensely rewarding rally programme with the Escort in the 1980s. European ventures into sportscar racing with the F3L at the end of the 1960s and the C100 in the 1980s, on the other hand, were scarcely worthwhile.

By that time there was an echo of 'Total Performance' in the parent Ford company, too, as Edsel Ford II announced 'the only front-door racing program in Detroit', though this was on a very modest scale compared with the multi-million dollar programme of the mid-1960s.

That programme had turned out to be pivotal, in USAC as well as endurance racing. It could be argued that an apparently limitless budget would inevitably lead to success, and in a European perspective it was argued that it was sheer extravagance to use a 7-litre engine to propel a two-seater car, although the subsequent evolution of supercars showed that a worthwhile number of people could be interested in two-seater road cars with engines rated at several hundred horsepower (indeed, Ford V8s were used in some mid-engined European supercars, and Ford was briefly

involved with one of the constructors, de Tomaso). One conclusion to be drawn from Ford's success was that a 7-litre pushrod V8 could be more effective than a race-bred 4-litre dohc V12, and that was anathema to many people in motorsport.

However, while that feeling may have been in the background, it could hardly be stated as a motive for the changes in the international regulations that were announced almost indecently soon after the 1967 Le Mans 24-hour race: in 1968, Group 6 Prototypes were to be subject to a capacity limit of 3 litres, while 5 litres was to be the upper limit for Group 4 Production Sports Cars (with the minimum production requirement reduced to 25 cars, which was to offer a great loophole!). One perfectly valid reason for these changes was the concern about rising speeds – at Le Mans, for example, where the worry was not so much about speeds approaching 220mph on the Mulsanne straight – although some designers were working at the limits of their aerodynamic understanding with cars at such velocities – as about speeds up to 180mph before drivers lifted for the right-hand bend after the pits. A chicane between White House and the pits had been mooted in 1966, and now Ford made their own incidental contribution towards reducing Le Mans speeds when they underwrote the construction of such a chicane (Virage Ford) on the approach to the pits. The 5-litre Group 4 cars envisaged under the new regulations were those using American pushrod V8s, and ironically this gave a new lease of life to the GT40.

9

New Lease of Life

3 litres and 5 litres in 1968

There was a widespread feeling that the new regulations for Groups 4 and 6 favoured the 3-litre Prototypes – even John Wyer held this opinion at the beginning of the 1968 season, reasoning that the bigger engines would give Group 4 cars an advantage only on the fast, straightforward circuits. So JW Automotive started work on a 3-litre Gulf Mirage, to compete against Porsche and, sooner or later, it was assumed, Ferrari, Alfa Romeo and even Ford, for in Britain Len Bailey had designed the F3L for this category. When it appeared, in coupe and spyder forms, that car was raced half-heartedly, leading John Wyer to speculate* that JW Automotive should have approached Ford of Britain with a proposition to take over the F3L, develop it and race it . . .

As it was, the Gulf team had to rely on the GT40, theoretically while their Len Terry-designed Mirage M2 was built and developed. In fact, the new car did not appear at any of the 1968 races, and the team depended entirely on the GT40 (with the exception of the non-championship race at Kyalami, when Ickx and Hobbs won in the single M1 the team retained). The first M2 was not completed until the summer, and was far from satisfactory in its initial tests, while the performance of its BRM V12 engine left much to be desired – had it not been for the Ford F3L, the Cosworth DFV might have been a preferred alternative . . .

The Certain Sound, published by Edita SA in 1981.

Meanwhile, unlike the Ford programmes for the GT40 and its successors, the Gulf commitment was spread fairly evenly over the Championship (two races were ignored, and the team was reinforced for Le Mans). Whereas the focus had been Ford versus Ferrari, it now switched to Ford versus Porsche. The cars proved to be evenly matched, 5-litre GT40s versus 2.2-litre 907 and later 3-litre 908 Porsches. But now the Ford team was the underdog, being run on a very restricted budget while their principal opponents were generously financed and equipped. In the field of competition, the basic GT40 design was ageing, although JW Automotive refined it to keep it competitive in Group 4.

Two of the team's front-line cars followed the Mirage, especially in weight-paring – the GT40P/1074 was actually a conversion of Mirage M10003, with the GT40 body lines. The third car run in Gulf's blue and orange colours was 1084, a rebuild of 1004 with a 1965 chassis and therefore heavier (it was used only occasionally). Gurney-Weslake heads made for a 10 per cent increase in power in the 4.7-litre V8, and contributed to reliability (in particular, gasket weaknesses became a thing of the past). Engine and gearbox lubrication systems were also improved, as were the brakes.

Later in the season, 5-litre engines were used, the 4,727cc unit being stroked to 4,992cc, and sufficient crankshafts were

95

The JWA-Gulf team's 1075 at Daytona (*left*), where it failed to finish in the 24-hour race, and at Brands Hatch (*below*), where Ickx is forcing his way between two Porsches on his way to the team's first victory of 1968. Brian Redman shared the driving in both races.

produced for the larger version to be homologated. It gave a little more power (just over 400bhp) and was much more flexible and reliable once – through the use of Cooper rings – it was persuaded to hold its water. The first engine was tested over a Le Mans cycle on a Gulf dynamometer. Outwardly the body was changed only to accommodate the wider wheels and tyres of the late 1960s, although the glassfibre panels were lighter and considerably strengthened with reinforcing carbonfibre, then very new and exotic. Overall, however, the GT40 gained weight and within the Gulf budget JWA could do little to combat this, for example by using alloys to replace steel components, as larger wheels and tyres and a fire extinguisher system offset savings. Geared for Le Mans, the 5-litre GT40 had a maximum speed of 205mph.

Private GT40s, too, were increasingly modified, but these were generally outrun in major races (Paul Hawkins' car perhaps being an exception, through sheer professionalism). During the season, several cars gained Gurney-Weslake heads to their engines, Tecalemit-Jackson fuel injection was fitted to one, while Hawkins used a Hewland gearbox in his red car, also an ex-Mirage 5.7-litre engine when race regulations permitted.

JWA took two 4.7-litre cars – an erstwhile Mirage and a new GT40 – to the early-season American races, with the strongest driver pairings so far seen in the history of the team. In practice at Daytona, Ickx in the new car lapped fractionally inside the lap record standing to a 7-litre car, at 119.370mph, 192.066km/h, and with Redman led the race for almost three hours. Hobbs and Hawkins also led, but the second car failed to reach half-distance. Both retirements were due to gearbox failures.

At Sebring, the cars were competitive in practice (Ickx was second fastest), and both led the race, but the Ickx/Redman car retired when the clutch failed after a spin, and the Hobbs/Hawkins car to all intents and purposes retired with a broken front suspension member after the Australian driver had left the track to avoid two spinning competitors (this GT40 was actually classified 28th). These failures in the early American races were a great setback to Championship aspirations because not only had Porsche won both, but the German effort was gathering strength – the 3-litre 908 was imminent – and some of the European races were on ideal 'Porsche' circuits.

In 1968, the race at Brands Hatch was the

The second Gulf GT40 was wearing small canard fins when Paul Hawkins and David Hobbs drove it to victory in the 1968 Monza 1,000-kilometre race.

first of the series to be run in Europe, and it coincided with the Le Mans test weekend. JWA sent a car to each, while there were Porsches aplenty for both occasions – 907s and the new 908 for Le Mans, well-tried 907s for the BOAC race. Two of the 907s shared the front row of the Brands Hatch grid with the Ford F3L; Siffert took pole with the first 100mph sportscar lap of the circuit, while in the hands of Spence and McLaren the Alan Mann-run F3L looked impressive. The Gulf GT40 was fifth-fastest, but in the race it was controlled with typical precision and driven faultlessly by Ickx and Redman. They kept it well-placed through the first half of the race, moved into the lead in the second half, and won by 22 seconds. Hawkins' AMGT-2 was 13th on the grid, but with Hobbs co-driving it finished the race fourth, behind two Porsches. One of the two new GT40s was a modest 11th, while the other (Drury's 1073, with fuel injection) retired, as did Prophet's older car.

Ickx spent the day before the race at Le Mans, where with a 4.7-litre engine he put in the fastest lap of the test weekend in 3min 35.4sec (139.88mph, 225.108km/h). This time could not reasonably be compared with those set in preceding years because of the new chicane, but the teams which attended at least learned that they could expect much greater brake wear in the 1968 24-hour race – as much as 20 per cent more, according to the technicians – as well as increased demands on transmissions through the number of extra gearchanges required (estimated to be 1,800 more for a GT40 running through the 24 hours). These tests also seemed to show that the larger engines would give Group 4 cars a distinct advantage on circuits with long straights.

That was confirmed at the next race, the Monza 1,000kms. In practice, Ickx was fastest, in 2min 57.0sec, more than two seconds ahead of Siffert in a Porsche 908. The race between GT40s and 908s was nicely balanced until the Porsches began to run into 'new car' problems. The Gulf team lost the Ickx/Redman car with rear-end damage, but

David Yorke counsels Paul Hawkins, who is about to take over the GT40 (1075) which was to finish third in the Nürburgring 1,000-kilometre race. On this occasion JWA did not put their strongest driving pair into one car (Redman was paired with Hobbs in the second entry) and the Ickx/Hawkins car was destined to finish behind a pair of Porsche 908s, the second of which was only 50 seconds ahead of the GT40 at the finish.

On a very wet day at Spa-Francorchamps, the Ickx/Redman GT40 (1075 again) trails a commendably flat plume of spray on its way to victory in another 1,000km race.

Hawkins and Hobbs brought the new car through to win. Piper and Salmon were second at one stage in the Strathaven GT40, but this car retired with engine failure (as did two other GT40s), while Drury crashed.

Porsche won the Targa Florio, which Wyer ignored, and the Nürburgring 1,000km race, and these victories gave the German team a clear lead in the Championship by 48 points to 27. But Porsche did not dominate at the Nürburgring as might have been expected, although in practice Rolf Stommelen did get just below the sportscar lap record (and that was remarkable as it had been set by Surtees before a chicane was built), while Ickx was just outside it with a time of 8min 37.4sec, almost five seconds slower than the best Porsche. In the race, Ickx held the GT40 well-placed through the opening phase, but co-driver Hawkins lost ground, then Ickx regained it, eventually to take third place for JWA, almost four minutes behind the winning Porsche. Hobbs and Redman were sixth in the other JWA car, while four independent GT40s were classified and two more retired.

Jacky Ickx and Brian Redman ran away with the next 1,000km race, on a miserably wet day at Spa. In dry conditions the outcome might have been different, for in practice the Ford F3L had the legs of everything else. As it was, Ickx lapped the field in 21 laps and, although marginally slower, Redman held this advantage through his stint to the 46th lap, leaving Ickx to reel off the next 25 laps to score a convincing victory. For this race the JWA team used its 'reserve' GT40, the overweight 1084, which handled poorly – it even looked wrongly set up – but was nevertheless driven through to fourth place by Hawkins and Hobbs. Independent GT40s were eighth and ninth, but three others crashed (Salmon's landing upside-down after crossing a bank).

The Spa result meant that Porsche had to take the new six-hour race at Watkins Glen seriously, and that JWA had to add it to their schedule. The GT40s were run with 5-litre engines, which gave a little more power and a greater advantage to drivers in a wider effective rev band. Although Siffert took pole for Porsche with a 908, his lap in 1min 10.2sec being six-tenths faster than Ickx' best, the

Privateers. *Above:* Paul Hawkins, who was very successful in secondary events with the erstwhile Alan Mann AMGT-2, revised to Group 4 specification. The wide wheels used on this car at the Silverstone International Trophy meeting and elsewhere necessitated the bulge over the spare wheel in the nose. *Left:* Terry Drury, seen here at Spa in 1073, fitted additional spoilers at front and rear, while David Prophet, pictured *below* at the Nürburgring in 1002, settled for small nose fins. All these cars are running without glassfibre panels over the sills.

Most private owners of GT40s, however, like Eddie Nelson, seen here at the Nürburgring, tended to run their cars without any aerodynamic aids. The car is 1009.

Porsche effort collapsed within an hour of the start and at half-distance the two GT40s were in a commanding position. So commanding, in fact, that after the car he shared with Bianchi had made two unscheduled stops, Ickx was able to turn a blind eye to 'Easy' pit signals, make up a two-lap deficit, and overhaul the Hawkins/Hobbs sister car. That led to rare friction within the team, but the result opened up the Championship.

For this, the best five results for a team were to count; JWA and Porsche each had four victories, so that 1968 Championship was to be settled on the basis of outright victories while other points scored became superfluous. The postponed Le Mans race became all-important. Both teams could have afforded to ignore the Austrian Grand Prix at Zeltweg, for as a 500kms event it counted for only half points in the Championship, but Porsche did contest it and won, with two 908s finishing five laps ahead of Paul Hawkins in his red AMGT-2.

French national politics had led to the Le Mans 24-hour race being postponed to late September, which meant a start at 3pm instead of the traditional 4pm, and a longer night to make extra demands on electrical systems. The standard of the entry was not high – the new regulations had seen to that – but for the first time Porsche went to the race with an excellent chance of an outright victory, while there was also the possibility of a Ford hat-trick. On paper, a pair of 5-litre

Lolas, or a 3-litre Matra, or the team of 3-litre Alpine-Renaults might have appeared to be in contention, although the reality was that these cars did little more than add interest to an entry list dominated by independent entrants.

JWA was under pressure, but confident in the 5-litre car, despite the fact that the longest run by a GT40 at Le Mans had ended after 19 hours (only at Daytona, in some respects less testing than Le Mans, had GT40s lasted for 24 racing hours). Moreover, Ford had unwittingly tilted the odds against a third Le Mans victory, for their chicane made extra demands on an already overstretched transmission. Ford support for the team was scanty, although there had been a little from the British company through the season.

A third car (1076) was added to the team as Gulf sought safety in numbers; this new car was built to the standard of the pair used regularly through the year (1074, the erstwhile Mirage, and 1075). One was run with a 'dry deck' engine supplied from Dearborn (in this version the water transfer ports were welded-up), otherwise the specification was unchanged and the team relied on painstaking preparation. There was, however, a driver problem, for Redman had been out of action since an accident in the Belgian Grand Prix and Ickx had been injured in the Canadian GP. Eventually, Muir and Oliver were enrolled for the third car, while Rodriguez returned to be paired with Bianchi.

Porsches dominated practice, the GT40s

In 1968, GT40s were not prominent at the front of the Le Mans line-up and they set off gently behind a flock of Porsches. Of the three JWA cars – Nos 9, 10 and 11 – only the Hawkins/Hobbs entry has moved in this picture.

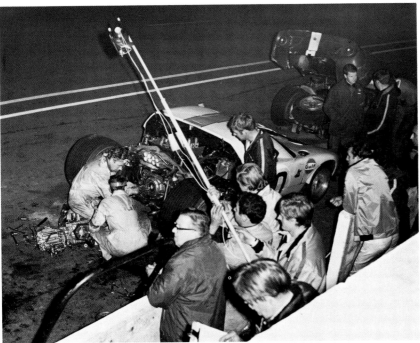

A midnight clutch rebuild delayed the Hawkins/Hobbs car at Le Mans, but the work was all to no avail as the car was retired soon afterwards with valve trouble.

Pedro Rodriguez and Lucien Bianchi were destined to give Ford their third consecutive Le Mans victory in 1968. Here their GT40 is leading the Hawkins/Hobbs car, with a Porsche sandwiched between them at the new Virage Ford.

Pit work for the winner. Beside the left front wheel, David Yorke supervises operations as Ermanno Cuoghi makes ready with the wheel hammer and John Wyer watches from the extreme left of the picture. In the lower picture, Rodriguez makes way for Bianchi during a refuelling stop as Wyer, to the left of Yorke, keeps an eye on the adjacent Porsche pit.

The architects of victory. John Wyer, Grady Davis, David Yorke and Jacky Ickx in session inside the Gulf motorhome early in the 1968 season. Ickx was to become one of the great endurance drivers of all time.

lapping slower than the single JWA car at the spring test weekend, and they were also slower than the German cars on the Mulsanne straight. Wyer estimated that in good conditions an average lap time of 3min 42sec would be fast enough to ensure victory over 24 hours (in poor weather around half a minute slower); 6,000rpm was set as the limit in intermediate gears, but up to 6,500rpm was allowed in top. Rodriguez put in the fastest practice lap in a GT40, his 3min 39.8sec being uncomfortably close to Wyer's race average target, while in the other JWA cars Hobbs lapped in 3min 41.8sec and Oliver in 3min 44.6sec. The three fastest times overall were set by Porsche 908 drivers, Siffert (3min 35.4sec, and reaching 200mph on the straight), Stommelen and Elford. The other Group 4 cars, a pair of Lolas, were well off the pace, but the Matra was competitive and fifth fastest.

As the race started, the Porsches romped away, and after an hour the leaders lapped the Rodriguez/Bianchi GT40 in fifth place, for it

had stopped early for dry tyres. Mairesse had crashed the Claude Dubois GT40 when he tried to close a door on the first lap, while after 11 1aps Muir started a three-hour dig to get his car out of the sand at Mulsanne (he succeeded, but that car completed only two more racing laps as its clutch was cooked).

As daylight began to fade, the Porsche situation was less secure – the JWA Fords moved up to third and fourth, and by the time it was fully dark Rodriguez and Bianchi led, with Hawkins and Hobbs in second place. Later in the evening, routine pit stops let a Porsche into the lead, but that lasted only briefly, and for most of the night Rodriguez and Bianchi led. The sister car fell back with clutch trouble, and eventually the clutch had to be replaced – this cost an hour and a half, and then after another 20 laps the car's engine failed.

At half-distance the surviving GT40 was four laps ahead of the second car, the Matra, and it was being driven carefully as the rain returned. By dawn it was seven laps ahead of a

Doors cut into the roof made the GT40 an ideal vehicle for drivers celebrating a victory. In this case Paul Hawkins and David Hobbs seem preoccupied with dodging the champagne after winning the 1968 Monza 1,000km race.

Despite the great success awaiting them, David Yorke and John Wyer appear less than confident at Le Mans in 1968 . . .

2-litre Alfa Romeo T33 that was swopping second place, pit stop by pit stop, with the Matra. By noon on Sunday, when the Ford still had a lead of seven laps, second place was held by a Porsche again. The race seemed to be a rerun of 1967 as a Ford with a commanding lead cruised towards the end of the 24th hour . . .

At the end of each of the last seven hours the Ford's average speed varied by only 0.177mph. Lucien Bianchi took the flag, although Rodriguez had hoped for this honour – perhaps as a reward for a restrained drive which then seemed so out of character? The winning car covered 2,767.02 miles, 4,452.88 kilometres, at 115.29mph, 185.536km/h, was fourth in the Index of Thermal Efficiency and 10th in the Index of Performance.

This was an outstanding triumph for John Wyer and his team, for Gulf, and for Ford – the Championship went to Ford as the manufacturer, and the name on the Le Mans record of winners was also Ford. The company had put an enormous effort into the GT40 series, so although its interest in the 1968 races had been minimal, it was no less than justice that it should receive this unexpected dividend.

The potential of the five-year-old GT40 had at last been realized, when it should have been considered obsolescent. The later cars departed little from the original concept, and the model had become reliable as well as rugged, but however it may have appeared in the first half of the 1960s, it was a bulky, heavy and outdated car by the standards of the late 1960s.

That it should have been so successful at the highest international level after Ford's withdrawal was surprising, and a tribute to John Wyer's faith; that it should appear again as a leading contender in 1969 would have seemed most improbable had the possibility been suggested in the late summer of 1967.

10

Wheel-to-wheel Le Mans

Nail-biting in 1969

The JWA-Gulf team had to bring their tried and trusted GT40s out again in 1969 for, although the Ford was apparently outclassed, progress towards raceworthiness in the Mirage M2 was painfully slow. So when the GT40 could have been expected to serve a season in genteel decline in the hands of private entrants it was raced in several Championship events by a front-line team. Maturity was an asset in that the car's habits were known and its behaviour on fast circuits was impeccable, while the economy of its 5-litre engine meant that it could run through a fast 1,000km race with one stop fewer than its 3-litre rivals.

The JWA cars had been immaculately maintained, but were little modified. The possibility of fuel injection was considered early in 1969 but set aside, and the 'dry-deck' engine was used – at first. Probably too much was read into its success at Le Mans, for the Sarthe conditions in September had not been typical; because the night had been wet and cold, and the car had not been under pressure on Sunday, coolant temperatures had remained low. It transpired that this engine could be relied on only in these odd conditions, at least as far as endurance racing was concerned, for it had been used successfully in TransAm saloons.

At one stage it seemed possible that a new 5-litre Ford engine might become available, but the possibility soon faded, and with it any idea of building a batch of cars to be homologated. So JWA pursued the 3-litre alternative, together with others such as Ferrari and Matra, despite misgivings about the endurance qualities of GP-based engines and, more significantly, the winter rumours that became fact when Porsche unveiled the controversial 917 at the Geneva motor show in March. A company like Ford could have sponsored the construction of 25 5-litre cars for considerably less than the cost of their Mk II/IV programmes, but Ford had lost interest in sportscar racing. Porsche not only saw the loophole in the regulations, but the possibility of selling at least a worthwhile number of the 25 cars which had to be produced . . .

The Mirage programme continued in the face of disillusionment at the power outputs of BRM V12s, a high drag coefficient, and many lesser shortcomings. However, it had been designed to accept the Ford-Cosworth DFV as an alternative, and when these V8s eventually became available to JWA a DFV-powered Mirage appeared. It suffered the vibration problems that sportscar teams using the DFV and DFL a dozen years later were to experience, but late in 1969 an open Mirage M3 was competitive, and won a secondary race. However, that was almost academic, for months earlier Porsche had approached Wyer to run their 'official' 917 team in 1970 . . .

Meanwhile, for the early-1969 races in America, JWA had no alternative to the GT40s. At Daytona, the pair were eighth and ninth fastest in practice (Ickx 1min 54.5sec and

Hobbs lmin 55.3sec, compared with an overall fastest time of lmin 52.2sec by Elford in a 908). But as the Porsche 908s fell out during the race, the reliability theory seemed to be holding good – at half-distance the 5-litre GT40s led, and at a higher average than the 7-litre Fords had achieved. But a block which cracked down a bore put one out after 420 laps and the engine of the other was failing when a crash ended its race. The 'dry-deck' engines were abandoned.

For Sebring the team prepared one car (1075) with a fully-tweaked Gurney engine producing 460bhp, some 20bhp more than JWA's normal V8s. Nevertheless, the odds stacking against the ageing and heavy GT40s were again demonstrated in practice when the two Gulf cars were 11th and 12th fastest – under the lap record, but distinctly slower than a new Ferrari 312P, a flock of Porsches and a pair of Lolas. However, the Porsches soon flagged with a rash of chassis failures, one of the Lolas led but retired, and the Ferrari suffered a body damaging incident, overheating, excessive oil consumption and a minor fire. The team kept it running, but its stops cost time while the GT40s plugged

round. With an hour to go Oliver took the lead, Ickx took over from him, and the pair won by a lap. Hobbs and Hailwood in the sister car with the 'normal' engine had been better placed through the opening hours (throughout, this car was generally superior in lap times), but a stop to repair a wheel hub cost half an hour, and the same trouble led to its eventual retirement. Just one other GT40 started in the early-year American races – that seemed to confirm that the Ford was a fading force . . .

Back in Europe, JWA ran just one GT40 alongside a Mirage M2 in the BOAC race at Brands Hatch, then put the GT40s away until Le Mans. In this opening European race the Mirage retired after 2½ hours, while Hobbs and Hailwood worked their way up the leader board to finish fifth in 1074, and class winners, albeit 20 laps behind the leading Porsche. Sadler's GT40 was placed 11th, and the IGFA car was a modest 16th.

This car, which was driven by Helmut Kelleners and Reinhold Joest and later run under the *Deutsche Auto Zeitung* banner, proved to be the fastest and most successful GT40 run by a private-entrant team in 1969. It

The winning GT40 at Sebring in 1969, when it was shared by Jacky Ickx and Jackie Oliver. This famous car, 1075, won six major races, two of them at Le Mans, where it covered 5,873 racing miles.

The strength of the opposition. The DAZ GT40 is eighth in this line-up for the Nürburgring 1,000km race, having been outclassed in practice by Porsches, Alfa Romeos and a Ford F3L (No 7).

The achievements of Kelleners and Jöst in the DAZ GT40 during 1969 were overshadowed by the outright victories scored by the Gulf cars, but this late car (1081, seen at Le Mans heading the Galli/Widdows Matra) scored well in Championship races. It was later converted for road use.

was fourth overall in the Monza 1,000kms, 10th (just behind Sadler's car) at Spa, and sixth overall in the Nürburgring 1,000kms, where the GT40 had first run in a race in 1964. After Le Mans, Kelleners and Joest drove it to an excellent fifth place overall (first in Group 4) in the Watkins Glen Six Hours, and that proved to be the last mainstream race placing for a GT40. The last Championship race of 1969, the Austrian Grand Prix, saw the first victory for a Porsche 917, and that pointed very surely to the immediate future of endurance racing, and of course Group 4.

GT40s were raced through the final months of 1969, and beyond. While private entrants scored honourable placings in secondary events in Europe and Southern Africa there were no more victories for the GT40 after the high summer of 1969, and it was perhaps most unfortunate that both GT40s in the revived Tour de France retired early, for a long run in that fascinating string of hill-climbs and circuit events could have proved the 'GT' part of the designation. Willie Green reckoned he had GT40P/1010 well-placed as he came to the end of the 'rally' stages, with the quick circuit stages to come, when alternator failure led to retirement. The Ford France entry (1082) driven by Michel Martin also retired. Green felt that his co-driver, John Davenport, was perhaps not attuned to GT40 speeds; for his part, Davenport was obviously impressed by an early-morning test run on a British motorway, when Green used the headlights to flash warnings to dots in the distance . . . he then realized that the GT40 was geared for a 180mph top speed. Incidentally, a problem in the event was an intercom that was adequate in a contemporary rally car, but was overwhelmed by the V8 behind the GT40's crew. It is worth recording that in a very different age, GT40P/1002 was driven to win the 1994 Tour de France Retrospective . . .

The German team was efficient and exploited the economy of their GT40 to the full, and their performances suggested that the JWA team might have taken their GT40s to Spa with every chance of gaining a third successive victory, or to Monza with at least the prospect of a good placing. The team did not even attend the Le Mans test weekend, when the fastest time was recorded by Stommelen in a Porsche 917 (3min 30.7sec), and the only GT40 present, Martin's car, returned a modest 4min 23.7sec, and Lucien Bianchi, co-driver of the winning car in 1968, was killed when his Alfa Romeo left the road on the Mulsanne straight.

Few people really gave any of the five GT40s in the Le Mans line-up much more than an outside chance, save that they might achieve good placings on Sunday afternoon through stamina, for the 24-hour race is never wholly predictable and teams with reliable, healthy cars have reaped dividends from simply keeping them plugging along for the

Le Mans again, and 1075 (No 6) looks travel-stained as it heads away from the pits towards the end of the 24-hour race, while the Hobbs/Hailwood car (1076) receives attention.

full duration. The five included a JWA-Gulf pair (the car which won in 1968 and a newer one), the *Deutsche Auto Zeitung* car (promoted from the original reserve list because of its record in 1,000km races), Malcolm Guthrie's virtually 'as-new' 1009, rebuilt from the bare hull up by Alan Mann Racing and fitted with a TJ fuel-injected engine, and Peter Sadler's reliable 4.7-litre car; Martin's ESCA 5-litre car was a reserve, and its fate was settled when it ran its bearings in practice.

Apart from a host of Porsches, proven 908s and unproven 917s, the field included new 3-litre works cars from Ferrari, Matra and Alpine, and compared with these the GT40 was very old in the motor racing timescale. JWA team manager David Yorke felt that against the known 3-litre opposition his GT40s were in with a chance. He rated the two works Porsche 917s more highly: once their potential had been shown in practice he reckoned that if their drivers were constrained to lap 15 seconds outside their demonstrated capability, they must win.

That capability was shattering. In the first session Rolf Stommelen lapped in 3min 22.9sec (148.493mph, 238.976 km/h), faster than the record established with the Ford Mk IV before the chicane was introduced on the approach to the pits. In the final line-up, the best GT40s were 14th, 15th and 16th fastest: Ickx/Oliver, 3:37.5; Hobbs/Hailwood, 3:39.4; Gardner/Guthrie, 3:42.7. The Kelleners-Joest GT40 seemed slow at 3:51.1, but Sadler and Vestey did well to break four minutes (3:57.7) in the owner's dark blue 4.7-litre car (1010). The JWA team adopted a restrained approach – little would have been proved in 'going for a time' which necessarily would have been remote from Stommelen's – while there were worries about the engine in Guthrie's car, and so this was changed by Mann's mechanics. At the start it seemed almost inconsequential that Jacky Ickx should make a point about safety by strolling across the track, carefully fastening his safety belts and moving off last but one; 22 hours later those casually squandered seconds were to seem precious . . .

It was not surprising that GT40s were not among the early pace-setters; indeed it was surprising that two featured on the leader board as soon as they did. After an hour the JWA cars were 12th and 15th, at two hours 11th and 13th, at three hours 11th and 12th, at four hours seventh and eighth. That seemed realistic, as 908 and 917 Porsches traded the lead and Matras lurked in contention. Already the Guthrie car was out of the running, after a long pit stop when the radiator was changed, then another when a drive-shaft coupling was replaced (a repeat failure was to lead to its retirement in the fourth hour).

By half-distance the JWA cars were fourth (Ickx/Oliver) and fifth (Hobbs/Hailwood), eight laps behind the leading Porsche, but ahead of the Matras. Kelleners and Joest had moved steadily through to 10th place, but the Sadler/Vestey car which had run as high as 14th had retired in the ninth hour with a burnt-out alternator.

But the great Porsche onslaught, as strong as any which Ford had mounted at Le Mans, was falling apart just as shatteringly as the early Ford efforts. In the daylight of Sunday, after 16 hours, the 917 driven by Elford and Attwood was lapping at an easy pace, around 3min 40sec, with a five-lap lead over the 908 driven by Lins and Kauhsen. Then came the Ickx/Oliver GT40, a further three laps down, the 908 driven by Herrmann and Larrousse and the Hobbs/Hailwood GT40, which had been delayed while a fractured brake pipe was repaired and was four laps behind its sister car.

By mid-morning on Sunday both leading Porsches had made unscheduled pit stops. The 908 limped out into the race again in third gear, and Kauhsen failed to complete another lap as the box jammed. The 917 slowed as its transmission wilted, and eventually failed. With exactly three hours of the race still to run (there was a 2pm start and finish in 1969) a GT40 led at Le Mans again.

Close – incredibly close – behind it was the surviving works Porsche 908. A brake pad and tyre change on the GT40 let the Porsche into the lead, then a Porsche refuelling stop was enough to give the lead back to the GT40. The race average started to increase again, the lead – so often measured in laps in the final hours at Le Mans – was counted in seconds, and fractions of seconds.

Jacky Ickx is shown the chequered flag after winning a gripping battle with Hans Herrmann and his Porsche, seen only a matter of yards behind after 24 hours.

Ickx and Oliver acknowledge the applause of the Le Mans crowd, who have been witness to one of the most exciting episodes in endurance racing history. Just over 24 hours earlier, Ickx had pointedly walked, rather than run, across the track to his car in a gesture against the dangers of setting off without being properly strapped in.

The final refuelling stops came with about an hour and a half to go, Ickx staying in the GT40 and Herrmann taking over the Porsche from Larrousse. Driver ability was now an important factor, and with less than an hour to go Ickx also enjoyed a little help from Hailwood, who kept between the leading GT40 and the Porsche for a couple of laps (the fact that Hailwood also got the better of a battle for third with Piers Courage in a Matra 650 through this phase tends to be overlooked).

Through the final hour the two cars raced nose-to-tail, even wheel-to-wheel, passing and

Improbable adventure. The Ford France entry for Martin and Samon was one of the two GT40s in the 1969 Tour de France.

The solitary JWA entry in the 1969 BOAC 500 at Brands Hatch, where it was driven into fifth place by Hobbs and Hailwood. As ever, Yorke closely supervises a pit stop, while 1074 shows off the spare wheel position.

repassing. Jacky Ickx and Hans Herrmann fought out their memorable duel to the end, Ickx making up in the corners for his car's outright speed disadvantage, losing and regaining the lead on the final lap. At the finish he was ahead by something like 100 yards after the most dramatic hour in Le Mans history.

Third place fell to the other JWA car, by the slightly more generous margin of just over a mile, while the ever-consistent *Deutsche Auto Zeitung* car was sixth. Curiously, in 1969 the drivers of the winning car were awarded *The Motor* Trophy for the highest-placed British car, for which the ACO had apparently considered the self-same GT40 not to be eligible in 1968!

The bare facts were that Ickx and Oliver covered 3,105.757 miles, 4,998.00 kilometres at 129.406mph, 208.250km/h, while Herrmann and Larrousse covered 3,105.682 miles, 4,997.88 kilometres. The three Fords were first, second and third in the Index of Thermal Efficiency, and fifth, sixth and ninth in the Index of Performance.

Three of the five GT40s which started had finished the race – at the end of its Le Mans career, this was the best showing ever for the type in the *Grand Prix d'Endurance*, the race for which it was conceived in 1963. In six years in the front line at Le Mans, 44 Fords had started, and nine had finished. The Fords won four of their six races and, with a programme started from scratch, this cannot be rated less than splendid. Ford GT40s were raced after June 15, 1969, but never again by a leading team at Le Mans. So it is appropriate that the story of Ford's 'Total Performance' endurance racing should be ended with its culminating Le Mans race, even if that victory was gained by an independent team. In the course of the Ford sportscar programme some superb road-racing machines were built; and those 1968 and 1969 victories at Le Mans firmly established the GT40 as an outstanding classic sportscar.

11

The Road Cars

Setting a supercar standard

Ford kept faith with a clause in the Prototype regulations by offering series-production GT40s for sale, although never in large numbers, and never through normal Ford dealers: all orders were passed through Dearborn before being executed by Slough, where all the production cars were built. These included 31 road cars, many of which crossed the Atlantic, although few got onto American roads and at least some eventually found their way back to Europe. In addition, several cars originally completed for circuit use, including one of the 'pre-homologation series', were privately modified for road use, and the cars completed in the 1980s and 1990s had road specifications. On the other side of the coin, and perhaps justifying claims that the GT40 was a true sportscar, the prototype road car, GT40P 1013, was raced when it was virtually in road-going condition in 1969 – it had some 50,000 road miles on the clock when owner Willie Green drove it to Portugal to run (and finish) in the Villa Real Six Hours.

The company's brochures were not lavish, and the two-fold colour broadsheet headed *This car you have to be measured for* had a restrained text, which departed slightly from fact to build on then-recent success in the implication that it derived from the Mk II:

'THE BESPOKE CAR. The thing to keep in mind is that the Ford GT40 is something very, very special in the way of cars. So special, in fact, that

you need to be measured for it, just as a tailor measures you for a bespoke suit. If you absolutely insist, of course, you can have one off the peg, but it would be rather like ordering something from Savile Row through a mail-order catalogue.

Far wiser and better to do the thing properly, and go along for a personal fitting. After all, when you are buying one of the sleekest, swiftest, most powerful machines ever to come on the market, you want to be sure – and Ford wants to be sure – that it's tailored exactly right. Only a personal visit can guarantee this.

Unless you have just dropped in from the far side of the moon, it will be unnecessary to point out that this is the car which created a sensation when it came in 1st, 2nd and 3rd in the 1966 Le Mans 24-hour race.

Naturally the domestic version has had to be de-tuned, because the Le Mans machine was race-bred, and would be altogether too formidable for anywhere outside a race circuit.

Special exhaust silencers have been developed, and softer brake linings incorporated. There has also been a 25 per cent reduction of the shock absorbers' stiffness.

But the overall performance figures still speak volumes. Output is a very smooth 335bhp at 6,250rpm, which gives a top speed of 164mph and maximum gear speeds of 1st . . . 58mph, 2nd . . . 90mph, 3rd . . . 127mph, 4th . . . 142mph, Top . . . 164mph.

SPACE AGE LINES. Externally, the road version of the GT40 looks little different from its Le Mans sister. It is just 40 inches high, and driver and passenger sit in a semi-reclining position, following modern practice in all racing and the best Grand Touring cars. Headlights are enclosed within the

FAV production cockpits. Illustrated on the opposite page are the somewhat spartan circuit GT40 and, *below*, the road car – tidier, padded and, slightly incongruously, with a cigar lighter and a multi-function indicator, lights and horn control in place of the switches to the right of the steering wheel. The right hand had to move only a short distance to the gear lever, which was short, light and positive to use – virtues which offset its inconvenience when entering or leaving the car. Forward visibility was good, although the pillars seemed thicker than they actually were because of their angle, but there were vast blind spots at the rear and external mirrors were absolutely essential. On this page, the Mk III is seen in both left-hand and right-hand drive form. The use of cheap stock components was widely criticized, as were the adjustable seats in place of the GT40's fixed seats.

117

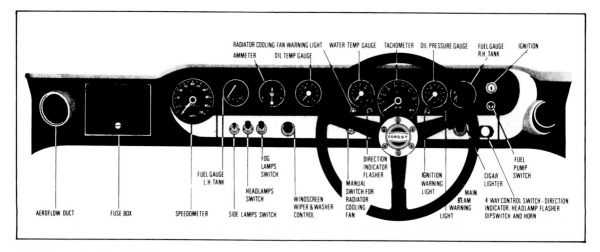

RADIATOR COOLING FAN WARNING LIGHT WATER TEMP GAUGE TACHOMETER OIL PRESSURE GAUGE FUEL GAUGE IGNITION
AMMETER OIL TEMP GAUGE R.H. TANK

FOG DIRECTION FUEL
LAMPS INDICATOR PUMP
SWITCH FLASHER SWITCH
FUEL GAUGE MANUAL IGNITION CIGAR
L.H. TANK SWITCH FOR WARNING LIGHTER
HEADLAMPS RADIATOR LIGHT MAIN 4 WAY CONTROL SWITCH - DIRECTION
SWITCH COOLING BEAM INDICATOR, HEADLAMP FLASHER
AEROFLOW DUCT FUSE BOX SPEEDOMETER SIDE LAMPS SWITCH WINDSCREEN FAN WARNING DIPSWITCH AND HORN
WIPER & WASHER LIGHT
CONTROL

The facia panel of the GT40. As can be seen on the preceding pages, the speedometer was angled towards the driver and therefore was not so far outside the arc of a normal instrument scan as its position might suggest.

bodywork and Perspex covers retain the sleek, space age lines.

Inside, nothing has been spared in the way of comfort and convenience for driver and passenger. Standard upholstery is black, and the floor and door sills are covered with deep carpet and thick underlay. As one would expect with such a power unit, there is a comprehensive array of instruments, all angled towards the driver's eye. There is also a special windscreen wiper which was developed to operate at speeds of up to 200mph on the racing GT.

Aeroflow, the unique Ford ventilation system, is standard equipment, as is a thermostatically controlled radiator fan, a heater/demister and an engine compartment light.

PERSONAL CHOICE. When you go for your personal fitting, among other things the engineers will discuss with you will be the rear axle ratios and the gear ratios. You can choose your own from a wide range. The tyres are specially made by Goodyear and incorporate all the lessons this famous company has learned in its highly successful racing programme.

There are two aircraft patterned fuel cells, with a combined capacity of 31 gallons. Fuel is delivered to the carburettors by a heavy duty Stewart Warner electric pump. A special two-plate clutch and flywheel complete the transformation from a truly formidable track champion to a smoothly luxurious road car which is equally at home in city streets or on high speed motorways.'

The brochure listed some of the modifications. Among others, four Webers were used (and, incidentally, it seems unlikely

that the claimed 335bhp was honestly given by the engines installed in civilized GT40s) and there was a reversion to Borrani spoked wheels. The sequential ZF gearbox was retained, which meant that the right-hand lever had to visit every slot in the gate in turn on the way up or down. Small front-hinged opening sections of Perspex were introduced in the door windows. Luggage space was not provided, although panniers on either side of the exhaust were added on odd cars.

A Ford High Performance Dealers Handbook was to half-admit this shortcoming: 'Although essentially a high-performance grand touring competition car, the Ford GT has a limited luggage capacity. Two special heat-resistant lockers are incorporated within the engine compartment at the rear and will hold two reasonably-sized suitcases. At a later date a special U-shaped locker will be fitted with a capacity for at least three suitcases.' Promises, promises . . .

Contemporary rumours suggested that FAV looked into the possibility of a longer chassis, leaving the engine where it was, of course, and creating space for luggage behind the seats (accessibly through small side hatches), or with a 2ft extension making space for a 2+1 layout. Either would also have moved the source of noise further from the seats, and perhaps have allowed for soundproofing. As it was, there was little insulation against noise as the engine was very close to the back of the

Above: A studio photograph of the first right-hand-drive Mk III (1102), taken as it was completed at the beginning of 1967. *Below:* The Mk III on the road. The reprofiled nose, amended headlamps and front overriders are clear identification features. A luggage container in the extended tail ran across the car, above the gearbox, with a modified exhaust system below it.

Luggage boxes in the GT40 had to be located in a rather warm and inaccessible area!

cockpit (a proximity that became even more apparent with the carburettor fires that sometimes added excitement to starting, and gave real meaning to 'firing up').

If GT is anglicized to read 'Grand Touring', there is an implication of certain qualities. In that the road-going GT40 lacked some of these it was not a grand touring car. The basic body saw to this: it was not habitable for real touring – however exemplary it might have been for fast motoring – for it was difficult to get into, and out of, tended to be noisy and hot, had enormous rearward blind spots, and lacked accommodation for even the smallest weekend bag.

But none could deny that the GT40 was a sportscar, with all the implied performance, in speed and acceleration, in roadholding and general feel. In 1968, *Motor* obtained the following acceleration figures with a well-maintained and healthy car at the MIRA proving grounds: 0-40mph, 3.2sec; 0-60mph, 5.3sec; 0-80mph, 7.7sec; 0-100mph, 11.8sec; 0-120mph, 15.9sec. Moreover, it was very flexible in top gear – *Motor* was able to time

acceleration in top from 20mph (20-40mph, 4.1sec, and at the other end of the scale, 100-120mph, 4.8sec), and it was possible to draw away from rest in top. The journal agreed that the maximum speed was around 160mph.

Denis Jenkinson borrowed Ford's press car (GT40P/1013) for a week in 1966 and recorded his impressions from an enthusiast viewpoint in *Motor Sport*:

'I thought the E-type Jaguar had acceleration from 80-130mph, but now I have to alter my sense of values, and the handling of the Ford makes it all so safe. Known local bends that the Jaguar can accelerate round in the upper 80s were taken easily at 120 and still accelerating. One of my prerequisites for high-speed motoring is to have enough reserve of horsepower and torque at 100mph to be able to stamp on the accelerator and surge forward so that you are quickly past an impending change of road traffic conditions. I have put the Porsche 911 and 911S aside because they do not reach my requirements, and I have felt the Jaguar to be adequate in this respect. The Ford makes the Jaguar seem dull and woolly, even in 5th gear . . .

Getting this sort of performance is no great

problem these days, but getting it as safely, smoothly and confidently as the Ford GT40 does is a new conception of motoring, and it makes you really appreciate the modern racing car, for in all mechanical respects as regards ride, suspension control, cornering power, steering and braking this road-equipped GT40 was identical to the Group 4 racing version. When you drive it fast over undulating roads at speeds in excess of 110mph the suspension and shock absorbers are working superbly, the engine is smooth, the steering light and unbelievably accurate ...

When the Ford empire set up its small specialized factory at Slough and called it Ford Advanced Vehicles I thought it was a bit of a joke. After a week of motoring in a GT40 I can now appreciate that not only have they produced an Advanced Vehicle, but it is here today and is a new conception in motoring that must soon become commonplace.'

The Mk III was the definitive road-going version. Two prototypes and a first production run of 20 cars were planned, but this programme was curtailed, largely because of Federal Safety Regulations, and only the two prototypes and five production models were completed. This decision was probably made at an early stage, as apparently only eight sets of the special suspension uprights for this model were made. At least four of the cars were initially retained by Ford.

Company literature referred to the 'GT40 Mk III' as 'a two-seat high performance road car with unparalleled performance'. A splendid non sequitur appeared as a broadsheet copywriter departed a little from fact to introduce reference to race successes: 'Aerodynamically stable with low drag characteristics patterned after the world renowned Ford GT Mark II road race cars, which adds to the structural strength of the car'.

In the Mk III an attempt was made to overcome some of the admitted deficiencies in the GT40. The interior was 'designed for functional efficiency; including adjustable ventilated seats of unique design, center floor mounted gearshift lever and retractable seat belts with inertia reels'. Sound and heat insulation was generously added, and the trim improved. The nose was modified, with four headlights behind Perspex covers – the square Cibie lights of the GT40 were illegal in many US states – and the tail was enlarged so that some luggage space could be incorporated, but this was a somewhat crude 6cu ft box in a rather warm area, and in effect little more usable than that offered up in response to Appendix J of the FIA regulations governing the construction of racing versions.

Springs and shock absorbers were softer.

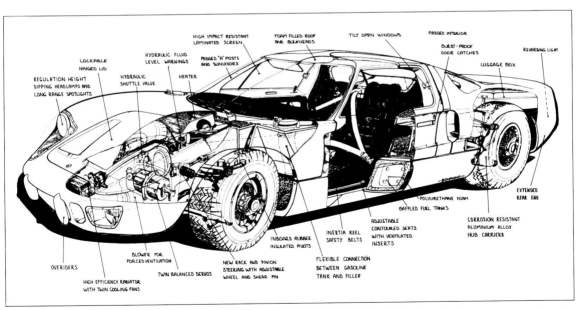

The Mk III exposed. A foam filling was used for the roof and the cockpit bulkheads as well as for the space surrounding the baffled fuel tanks. The spare wheel was carried on a sloping platform beneath a lockable hinged lid.

The most widely publicized customer for a Mk III was the conductor Herbert von Karajan. John Wyer and John Horsman demonstrate a novel use for the driver's door as they compile a specification for the famous musician. Or are they merely totting up the bill? Either way, von Karajan looks suitably amazed!

With the engine there was a reversion to a single Holley four-choke carburettor, while the V8 was detuned and rated at 306bhp (three of the cars had 302cu in engines). Because of the central gear lever, radiator pipes were moved to the sills, and tank capacity was reduced to 23 Imperial gallons (27.6 US gallons, 104 litres), with alloy tanks surrounded by polyurethane in place of the bag tanks – a practical improvement that was to be retrospectively applied to some GT40s.

That centre gearshift lever was a weak link, although it did make for easier access to the cockpit. As it had to be for a left-hand-drive car, the gear lever for the ZF five-speed gearbox was moved from the right-hand side of the cockpit to a conventional position, whence the linkage followed a necessarily tortuous path, and gear selection became less precise.

There were other shortcomings, and in particular the detail of furnishings and accessories was skimped as expediency dictated the use of proprietary components and parts from more mundane models, which seemed out of place in a high-priced GT car. Even the sound insulation was achieved cheaply, relying on thick padding in the cockpit, which incidentally soaked up any

water that leaked in (or simply fell straight in if a door was opened when it was raining!). Ford could – should – have learned from an example set by Graber, which was exhibited at the Geneva motor show in 1966, a year before the first Mk IIIs were produced. This car, 1033, was trimmed to a high standard and fitted with wind-up windows, whereas those on the Mk III were simply front-hinged. Ironically, 1033 was later converted for circuit use, and it is one of several GT40s that have been seriously damaged in fires, but rebuilt.

Roger Bell reflected in *Motor* in 1968: ' . . . the world is now richer by around one hundred gems of pedigree machinery' and ' . . . future generations will look back on Henry Ford II as a charitable sportsman when they jostle with open cheques for a vintage GT40'. With hindsight, that can be seen to have been a very safe prediction, and 15 years after the first road cars emerged from Ford Advanced Vehicles the asking price for a GT40 with no particular distinctions was more than a dozen times the original projected list price of £5,900 (around £7,000 by the time production was really under way in 1965, which just allowed an adequate mark-up on the proposed dealer nett price). Another 15 years on, when classic car values had recovered from a slump, the pre-auction valuation for an undistinguished and much-restored circuit-specification car was of the order of £130-165k.

Only a dollar price, $18,500, was quoted for a Mk III, when a circuit GT40 was priced at just over $16,000, while the original street GT40 had a $15,400 price tag.

The early reluctance to accept that Ford had produced a thoroughbred soon gave way to a recognition that the company had achieved just that, despite the use of an engine which the diehards protested was 'crude', and that save in the matter of luggage space Ford had marketed a high-performance mid-engined car while others were still working on the concept. Lamborghini, for example, first showed their Miura – which was to become a yardstick – at Geneva in 1966, and some 1,200 examples of that model were to be sold before production ceased in 1972. Moreover, the Miura's designer was to admit that the broad layout of the GT40 inspired the Lamborghini supercar. Does this suggest how well Ford might have done with a really refined derivative of the GT40?*

Could this have come to pass? Like so many histories, the GT40 story could include a chapter on missed opportunities, and comparisons with production figures for other supercars might have looked very different if one part of the 'Total Performance' concept had gone ahead. This envisaged networks of High Performance Dealers in Europe and North America, which would market the Ford GT (the '40' was sometimes discarded in the USA), Mustang GT-350, Cobra 427 and Cortina Lotus, to put into effect a company philosophy of 1965-66. Two decades, and several fuel and economic crises on, this almost has a period ring: 'Total Performance is not simply an advertising theme which will soon be obsolete. It is a merchandising platform for Ford Motor Company and Shelby American. One which follows the maxim "you can sell an old man a young man's car, but you can't sell a young man an old man's car". It is a well known fact that today's young people are overwhelmingly performance minded . . . the manufacture and marketing of competition cars is the logical outgrowth of Ford's Total Performance platform.'

The FAV-Shelby theme ran through extensive operating drafts. For example, European orders for the two Shelby models were to be processed through FAV. Although the GT40 was the star model – and carried a proposed dealer nett price exactly double the next most expensive on the list, the Shelby Mustang GT-350 (in both cases 'full competition model') – the volume would have come from Shelby. In little more than three years, Shelby American had evolved from a small garage operation to a thriving business, with a 96,000sq ft plant on the south side of Los Angeles International Airport coming into operation in March 1965, and capable of putting through 400 Shelby Mustangs and 50 Cobras per month.

The Shelby American High Performance Dealer chain existed, with more than 125 outlets nationwide. A European equivalent did not come into existence in the GT40's time, although the paper groundwork was thoroughly done, in all respects from dealer qualification to warranty terms for the models (for a road-going GT40 this was 4,000 miles, or 90 days). 'Because Special Vehicles appeal mainly to those customers who demand the ultimate in performance, handling and reliability, they can be produced only with meticulous care and in reliance on an orderly flow of firm orders' (FAV Special Vehicles sales agreement draft). This appeared at the time when Lamborghini was preparing the Miura for its first showing – perhaps Ford really could have achieved the same sales record with the GT40 . . .

Would-be Ford High Performance Dealers were given data – youth market figures,

---

*In circuit terms it became customary to refer to the GT Fords as 'the big Fords'. In fact, the wheelbase of all models was identical to that of the Ferrari 330P4, while in principal dimensions the production GT40s and the Mk II were slightly smaller than the Miura:
GT40 and Mk III: wheelbase 95in, overall length 168in, overall height 40.5in.
Lamborghini Miura: wheelbase 98.4in, overall length 171.6in, overall height 41.5in.

Pages 124 and 125 show a reproduction of Ford's surprisingly modest double-sided two-colour brochure for the Mk III.

HIGH PERFORMANCE ROAD OR TRACK CAR

The Ford GT 40 Mark III is a two seat high performance road or track car with unparalleled performance.
The car has exceptional road holding characteristics,
with tremendous stability, steering, and braking. A
luggage compartment in the rear section provides
6 cu. ft. of luggage space. Although the car is a high
performance car it is easy to handle in normal traffic.

INTERIOR: Is designed for functional simplicity;
included adjustable, ventilated seats of unique design;
center floor mounted gearshift lever and retractable
seat belts with inertia reels. The instrument panel
includes tachometer, speedometer, oil temperature
and pressure gauges, ammeter, water temperature
gauge, fuel gauge, switches and warning lights.

CONSTRUCTION: Structural foam sandwich chassis
and body construction with flat floor. Body is high
tensile reinforced fibre glass and has removable nose
and hinged access lid. The tail of the body is also
hinged for greater engine accessibility.

The side sills form the main structural members and
contain baffled fuel tanks. These fuel tanks are
surrounded by, and the hollow cavities uniting the
sills to the front structure and the double skinned
roof are filled with, high density polyurethane foam
to form sound absorbing beams of great torsional
and beam rigidity. This construction provides a
passenger capsule with exceptional strength.

STYLING: Aerodynamically stable with low drag
characteristics and patterned after the world
renowned Ford GT Mark II road race cars, which adds
to the structural strength of the car.

SUSPENSION: Front and rear suspension modified
for varying road conditions, driver reaction, and tire
profiles. Increased ground clearance, low friction,
low rate rubber inner pivots and sealed joints. Anti-
corrosion high tensile aluminum alloy hub carriers
with modified lugs. Suspension system is fully independent.

FORD GT40 MARK III

STEERING: Rack and pinion of a new design— available in either right or left drive models. The geometry allows immediate response to the driver's touch.

BRAKES: Disc brakes front and rear, 11.5″ dia. front and 11.2″ dia. rear. Dual master cylinders have individual large capacity reservoirs. The driver will get a warning from an indicator light on the instrument panel if the reservoirs have low fluid, excessive brake pad wear and/or rapid loss of fluid.

WHEELS AND TIRES: Wheels are 15″ Borrani wire spoke with light alloy rims, 6.5″ front and 8″ rear. Cast magnesium racing wheels are also available in 8.5″ front and 10″ rear. Tires are Goodyear Wet Weather Racing, 5.80 front and 7.00 rear.

CLUTCH AND TRANSAXLE: A Borg and Beck 8.5″

2-plate diaphragm spring unit clutch combines high torque capacity with low inertia.

ZF 5DS-25 FIVE-SPEED: A fully synchronized transaxle provides a wide variety of final drive and intermediate ratios.

FUEL SYSTEM: Tank capacity is 27.6 gallons, with a tank in the side sills of the car. These tanks are insulated from heat and noise by the polyurethane foam around them.

The fuel gauge will indicate the fuel level in either tank at the flick of a switch on the instrument panel. This switch also controls the electric fuel pump so that the fuel will be pumped from the tank indicated on the fuel gauge. Uniform performance is enhanced with a fuel pressure control device.

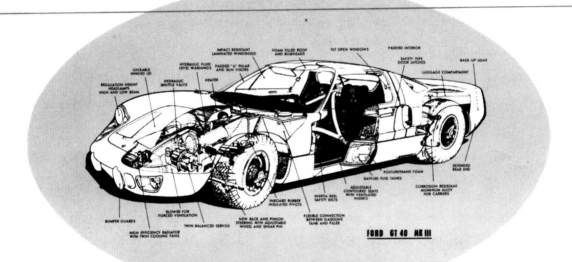

FORD GT 40 MK III

EXHAUST SYSTEM: Is designed to provide maximum efficiency without the complication of the crossover racing system. A transfer pipe is included in the system to reduce pressure interference caused by uneven firing impulses on each bank of cylinders.

COOLING SYSTEM: A fully ducted all copper radiator of 240 sq. in. face area provides efficient cooling for the engine.

Air flow through the radiator is provided by two thermostatically controlled electric fans positioned behind the radiator.

ENGINE: Cobra "289" V-8. The specifications are:

- Cobra OHV 289 cu. in. 90° V-8
- 306 bhp @ 6000 rpm
- 329 lbs./foot of torque @ 4200 rpm
- Bore 4.4005″
- Stroke 2.87″
- Compression ratio 10.50:1
- Cobra hi-rise intake manifold
- Holley 4-bbl carburetor (715 cfm flow rate)

- Solid valve lifters
- Die cast, polished aluminum "Cobra" rocker arm covers and air cleaner.
- Dual exhaust system.

GENERAL SPECIFICATIONS:

Wheelbase	95.3″
Tread	Front and rear 55.2″
Length	169.0″
Width	70.0″
Height	41.0″
Overhang	front 41.5″
	rear 32.2″
Approach Angle	17°
Departure Angle	23°
Minimum Ground Clearance	5.25″
Curb Weight (No Fuel)	2200 lbs.
Distribution	front 967 lbs. (45%)
	rear 1233 lbs. (55%)

These descriptions and specifications were in effect at the time of printing. The Ford Motor Company, whose policy is one of continuous improvement, reserves the right to change specifications or design without notice and without incurring obligation.

Much was made of this batch of cars prepared for shipment to the USA at the end of 1966, although most of them were to return to the UK.

motorsport attendances, enthusiast magazine circulation figures, and so on – to justify Ford's intention 'to tap this huge and growing market the Ford Division has undertaken its Total Performance concept'. As far as the GT40 was concerned, this philosophy was soon redundant – the 1966 Le Mans victory party in New York attracted 'outside' US companies to the programme and to Ford (it was lauded as an American victory), but that win seemingly failed to boost Ford's US car sales, GM sales were not dented, and the safety lobby began to swing opinion against sportscars. Some of the cars in a well-publicized batch shipped to Shelby American Inc in 1966 were returned to Europe . . .

But in marketing matters Ford has usually 'got it right', at least since the Edsel debacle, and although GT40 production was outside the mainstream, it could have absorbed disproportionate time if the High Performance Dealer network had been set up, and then had to be supplied. The basic idea could work for Ford, but at the right level and in the right quantities – that much was demonstrated later by the remarkable four-year run of the Advanced Vehicle Operations assembly line, which produced more than 13,000 Escort variants before it was closed early in 1975. The GT40 programme had transformed the company image; as a profit centre in realistic Ford terms, FAV was a non-starter . . .

126

A Ford promise of a boot extending across the back, above the exhausts, was fulfilled in the longer tail of the Mk III, although it was a primitive arrangement. The V8 engine seems almost insignificant . . .

Moreover, a sufficient demand probably did not exist for the car as it was at the time, and production slowed noticeably once the required 50 had been built, tailing off in 1967 when the last road cars were built at Slough. The design could have been refined, but it must be questionable whether the exercise would really have been worthwhile in Ford terms.

Almost as a postscript to this chapter, Mk IIs and – quite extraordinarily – Mk IVs have been adapted for road use – truly Le Mans cars for the street. The first Mk IV to be converted was J-3, acquired for Harry T Heinl from Kar Kraft, in poor condition but with masses of spares available at Holman &

Moody, where the rebuild was carried through under Freddy McCall, who had worked on the Mk IVs from 1966. Enhancement ran from a stereo radio to wood rubbing strips to protect the underside (the suspension was also modified, to increase ground clearance by 2in). The 7-litre engine was in detuned form, producing some 500bhp; with gearing unchanged from its Sebring 1967 ratios, the top speed was estimated to be 174mph.

A sister car, J-6, fourth at Le Mans in 1967, was converted by James M Glickenhaus in the 1980s, and in the late 1990s it was the only Mk IV registered for road use. By that time James had covered 'thousands of miles in it' on public roads.

THE EVOLUTION OF FORD MOTOR CO. EXPERIMENTAL AND SPORTS PROTOTYPE VEHICLES

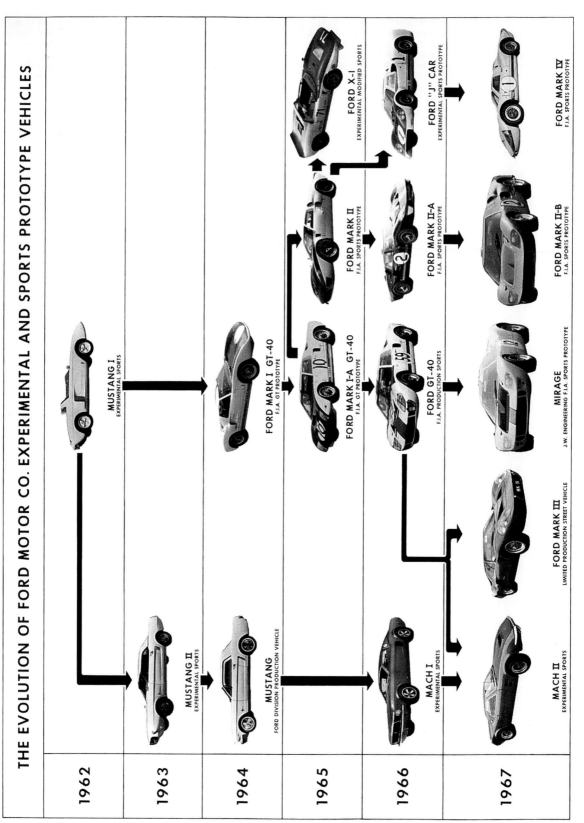

The GT40's place in the Ford family tree. As this chart demonstrates, Ford marketing people were keen to emphasise a connection between the racers and the company's experimental road vehicles during a period when Total Performance was their most powerful and effective slogan.

First race. The second GT40 (GT 102) was the first to start in a race, in the 1964 Nürburgring 1000km. *Above:* John Wyer (dark blue shirt, on pit counter) watches anxiously at a stop, perhaps waiting for a diagnosis from the crouching man at the rear, where weld failures led to the car's retirement after it had covered 213km. *Right:* Practice had gone well, for Phil Hill was second fastest, splitting the works Ferraris in the start line-up. The low sleek lines of the GT40 are emphasized by a Ferrari 250 GTO as Hill positions it before the start of a session.

GT 106 was the first 427-engined car, a Mk II in all but designation. Ken Miles is the driver in this 1965 Le Mans shot, taken during the car's only race.

Period piece. Graham Hill with Alan Mann at Goodwood late in 1965 during a press demonstration. The car (1008) was used extensively for this purpose before receiving repaints to resemble Le Mans winners for other show duties. Restored to original condition, it still serves Ford in this role.

Comparisons at the 1966 Spa 1000km race. The Essex Wire team GT40 (1026, *right*) is running without external mirrors, which was unacceptable to some race organizers. The principal identifying features of the Mk II run by Alan Mann Racing (1012, *below*) are the additional air intakes. This car also has a lip ahead of the nose-top outlet. Drivers are David Hobbs and Sir John Whitmore, respectively.

Below: The first GT40 to be raced by an independent team was 1002, entered by F English Ltd and driven at Silverstone in May 1965 by Richard Attwood (here seen following the little wall that lined the inside of Copse Corner).

The officials seem unhurried at the Le Mans start in 1966. The first four cars in the line-up are Mk IIs. Gurney has almost reached the door of No 3 (1047), but Miles is lagging behind as he makes for No 1 (1015). The next two are No 8 (Mann's XGT-1) and the eventual winner, No 2 (1046). Beyond the first of the Ferraris is the other AMR entry, XGT-2.

The triumphant 1-2-3 finish at Le Mans in 1966 was re-enacted in the morning before the start of the 1996 24-hour race. The Mk IIs were in their 1966 liveries and driven by their 1996 owners – George Stauffer of Wisconsin in the winning 1046, Bryan Mimaki of Los Angeles in 1015, which was second in 1966, and Ken Quitenz in 1016. This 1996 event was in the hands of Lee Holman and Jim Rose, who were at Le Mans in 1966 with the H&M and Alan Mann teams.

The atmosphere at the 1967 Le Mans test weekend seemed generally relaxed as David Piper trickled Mirage M10002 past the pits. This was the first public appearance on a circuit for JWA's slippery GT40 variant.

The Mk IV was a formidable racing machine, shamefully under-used by Ford – save that this car convincingly won at Le Mans in 1967. Only one other Ford finished, while 10 retired.

Gulf colours were to appear on several GT40s, and later replicas, but these are the 'real thing'. *Above:* Bianchi takes over 1075 from Rodriguez during their winning drive at Le Mans in 1968. *Left:* Le Mans preliminaries in 1969. No 6 is 1075 again, and it was to be driven to a second victory; No 7 is 1076, which was to finish third. Rival fuel company names are prominent, while 'Gulf' appears very discreetly on mechanics' overalls.

Above: Completed production GT40s in the sparse FAV Slough plant late in 1966. All are road cars, on Borrani wheels; 1067 is being pushed, 1066 is on the right. *Right:* Pristine Mk III, one of the four left-hand-drive cars, but British-registered during the three years it spent in the UK. The front-hinged window in the driver's door is open to its full extent. *Below:* This late Mk V (1141) was completed in 1993, to full race specification. The silver and black colour scheme suits its wide rear body section.

This early GTD40 looks the part. The legend on its flanks and badges on the wheels confirm its identity.

An immaculate ERA Replica Automobiles 'GT40' at Road America in 1994, waist-high to an official.

Ford's Mk III (1107) leads a GT40 procession past Goodwood House during the 1995 Festival of Speed. It is followed by a GT40 and a Mk V. The sun shining into the cockpit of this car gives the impression that it is a roadster, but it is actually a coupe running with the top sections of the split doors removed.

12

The Mk V

Extending the line

Genuine GT40s were rarely available by 1980, and when one did come on the market it could be expensive and its condition could well be questionable – broadly, cars had been built at Slough to fulfil an immediate purpose, and longevity or future 'classic' status were not taken into account. Enthusiast Peter Thorp sought one, failed to find a good rust-free car, and set out to build his own. His approach was wholly professional – his Safir Engineering company had built competent Formula 3 cars in the mid-1970s, and had run a modest GP effort before turning to Range Rover conversions, and he was close to John Willment, who was to become involved with Thorp's GT40 programme.

Thorp's first thoughts were to build a replica for his own use, but discussions with Willment led them to Dearborn to confirm their legal rights to the GT40 name and to an agreement to build more cars (originally a batch of 25 was proposed). A royalty was to be paid on each, and Safir was to pick up the chassis number sequence. In this, incidentally, allowance was made for the three JWA cars that were known to be stored in component form and were to be 'rediscovered' and built up by Bryan Wingfield in 1996-98 with the numbers 1087-1089. So Thorp's first GT40 was 1090, laid down in 1980 and completed in 1981; the sequence ran to 1100, then skipped over the Mk III numbers.

As well as the legal title, Thorp took over some jigs – others had to be created – and a set of body moulds. He was joined by Len Bailey, who had been a design engineer on the original Ford programme, Jim Rose, whose long association with the GT40 started with the Alan Mann team, and other GT40 mechanics from the 1960s. Bailey revised the design in some areas, to a degree to simplify it for Safir production. There was a fabricated rather than a pressed chassis, twin alloy fuel tanks to cut out the known weak point of rubber bag tanks, and suspension revisions to 1980s rather than early 1960s standards (but not far removed from the Alan Mann modifications of that decade), with new uprights and wishbone mounting points. A twin-plate AP clutch took the place of the rather heavy triple-plate unit, drive-shafts with constant-velocity joints – rather than inner 'doughnuts' and outer Hooke joints – were used, and AP 12in ventilated disc brakes better suited to road driving in the 1980s were fitted.

The chassis were treated with anti-corrosives, with much of the steel being zinc-coated, to overcome one shortcoming of the Slough-built cars, while by 1991 the body panels were in carbonfibre/Kevlar rather than the glassfibre of the 1960s cars. Better cockpit ventilation – deliberate ventilation, that is, rather than the draughts through joints and door edges in the forerunners – was provided, and with the generally higher build quality made for improved habitability.

This work was sufficient to justify the

Safir's first GT40 'Mk V' was an open-topped car, but it was to be followed by more conventionally styled cars with doors recessed into the roof in the familiar way.

'Mk V' designation, and as it was recognized by Ford as well as JWA, replicar manufacturers could use neither it, nor the 'GT40' name. The chassis plates were to be annotated 'J.W. Automotive Engineering Limited' and sales brochures carried JWA's address as sales through them were envisaged. But there was no Ford badging – perhaps product liability was a worry? The identity 'GT40' sometimes appeared on a 'go-faster' stripe on the flanks, as did 'Powered by Ford', but otherwise the only badging was a stylized 'GT40 MkV' on the magnesium wheels, which were cast from original BRM patterns.

Thorp reckoned that an aluminium monocoque could be a worthwhile improvement, and his first car had one comprising bonded panels in high-tensile manganese aluminium sheet, still with square-tube stiffening. Coupled with light honeycomb body panels, this led to a weight saving of the order of 100kg. He was to admit that 'circuit thinking' led to this, and that in practice the chassis could stretch and give a little on undulating roads – seams could spread and rivet holes become slightly oval – so this lightweight theme was not followed through the whole series. Normal Safir cars were fractionally lighter than the 1960s cars because of the tub, detail fittings and the twin alloy fuel tanks (which held 114 litres/25 gallons). The lightest steel chassis is 1099, extensively drilled by Jim Rose when he assembled this car; it weighed 285lb, including the fuel tanks, and

138

The first Safir car had a Mathwall-prepared 302 CID V8 engine with Gurney-Weslake heads fed from a single Holley carburettor, but the lower picture shows a later example, powered in this instance by a 289 engine with four Webers. The tyres of these two cars – Michelin XWX and Goodrich, respectively – were, of course, departures from the original GT40 specification.

The front end of the Mk V Safir, showing the large ventilated brake discs and wide crossflow radiator, with cooling fans behind it. The ends of the folded-sheet sills show another example of practical simplification, while the high quality of workmanship is evident throughout.

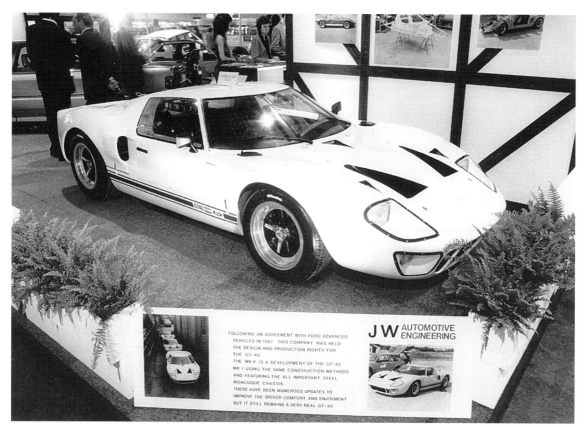

The Mk V on show, with a notice explaining its credentials. It is an early car, with closed bodywork (unlike the Safir prototype), and unusually there is a blue oval among the badges on the 'go-faster' strip.

A Safir fabricated chassis, showing the extent to which the doors were cut into the roof. Generous anti-corrosion treatment was a distinct improvement on the FAV cars.

Jim Rose's 1099 with everything open. Its chassis (*below*) carried the 'added lightness' theme to an extreme and inevitably invites 'Swiss cheese plant' comments. This immaculate car was delivered in 1987, for Rose to complete, and it has clocked up negligible mileage.

Detail departures from the original in the Mk V cockpit include the square-topped central spine and, of course, the mandatory seat belts. The steering wheel carries a Mk V badge.

the dry weight of the complete car is only 1,860lb. In a nice conceit, an 'L' has been added to the designation, and the registration number MKV 40 is genuine . . .

Peter Thorp's 1133 was the first of the aluminium-chassis cars, and it also had a lightweight carbonfibre body. The overall weight of this 1991 car was 1,900lb. Only one other aluminium-chassis car was built.

The first Mk V was a roadster, and two more were to be built, together with some cars which had small removable roof sections ('split doors'). To maintain rigidity, the open cars were reinforced at the A posts and rear bulkheads. Their cockpits were remarkably free of buffeting – a small panel added behind the top frame of the windscreen helped – and of course the high rear window which formed the engine deck was retained.

The 'split window' first seen in 1985 was an alternative to the roadster style, almost providing a Targa top, and a welcome innovation for tall drivers. The main side windows were retained, with small removable top sections on each side of the steel centre spine (Safir even provided small pockets to stow the top pieces).

Outwardly, the Mk V was faithful to the original, and so was the interior. Sensibly, Safir avoided the complication of the left-hand-drive Mk III and its centre gear-lever, so all Mk Vs were in right-hand-drive form, with the lever as well as that wide sill having to be negotiated on entry and exit. The instrument layout followed the original, and the Smiths Industries dials were identical.

The first Ford V8s to be used were mainly 289 CID (4.7-litre) units, prepared by Mathwall and rated at 350bhp. However, the first car had a 302 CID V8 engine, and this soon became the normal fitment (a few Mk Vs were sold as rolling chassis). Mathwall increased the stroke of this unit to give a 5.3-litre capacity, and with a four-barrel Holley carburettor the quoted output was up to 400-425bhp by 1991. Special versions gave up to 450bhp, with as much torque as some people reckoned the ZF 5DS-25/2 gearbox could handle (although developed for the BMW M1, this unit was closely similar to that fitted by JWA). The 302 CID engine in 'road/race' trim had Gurney-Weslake cylinder heads, Cosworth aluminium pistons and Carello connecting rods, a dry-sump system, four Weber 49IDA carburettors and electronic ignition – some of that may sound a little old-fashioned in this fuel-injection age, but it still made for a really high-performance engine.

Nevertheless, some American and Japanese customers wanted more, and a few cars were fitted with 494 CID (8.1-litre) aluminium V8s, which could be tuned to give claimed power outputs approaching 600bhp. That was really too much for the 15in tyres, but then perhaps their drivers were sensible, or not brave enough to use the available brute force – as it was, one claimed to have reached 185mph (300km/h) on a public road, and the car's theoretical top speed was 219mph (350km/h).

Outwardly, these cars were distinguished by two prominent (and inelegant) carburettor air intakes above the tail. They were noisy to the

Peter Thorp's lightweight Mk V roadster. The engine is a 5.3-litre V8 with Holley carburation.

point of being anti-social in a residential area. But, as with the small-block Mk Vs, the crossover exhausts meant that the sound was sheer music to an enthusiast . . .

Most of the first batch of Mk Vs were built at Safir's Byfleet shops, then assembly was undertaken by noted GT40 enthusiast and restorer John Etheridge, whose association with the type started in FAV days. Component acquisition was carefully controlled, in cost as well as quality aspects. The chassis were built by Kerry Adams (Adams-McCall Engineering, noted for historic racing car restorations).

The first batch of 25 Mk Vs was well received, and the programme was extended to 50 chassis. But sales slowed markedly as market conditions changed, cheaper 'replicars' became widely available, and the value of classic cars of every make and type slumped. In an episode that would have been familiar to some European specialist constuctors through half a century, a US distributor failed to take all of an agreed batch of Mk Vs. The early cars had sold for just under £50,000, but later in the 1980s prices had risen to more than double that figure, and then had almost doubled again by the next decade, when sales slowed dramatically (just three cars were completed in 1993, and one in 1994). So the target build was cut back to 40 cars, some of the last being high-specification lightweight or racing-specification types. The last of all 'official' GT40s, GT40P 1145, was still to be completed as this chapter was written . . .

13

The Production Record

Ownership and identification

The Ford Advanced Vehicles plant at Slough was small, having a floor area of approximately 16,000sq ft – sufficient for the development and assembly work that was carried out there – and, in the FAV days, a staff of around 45, working in conditions far removed from a normal automotive assembly line. Many were former Aston Martin employees, for apart from the John Wyer connection, Aston's move from nearby Feltham to Newport Pagnell almost coincided with the establishment of FAV.

A list of just over 100 of these Fords is by no means straightforward. Some cars that were apparently beyond repair after accidents have been rebuilt, whereas odd examples that were only lightly damaged have 'disappeared' (and it is not unreasonable to assume that major parts were used in later cars), while some early cars were rebuilt to later specification, with new chassis plates. GT40 write-offs are difficult to quantify, and there must also be misgivings about 'lookalikes', but it seems that only eight and maybe fewer cars have been lost for all time:

GT40/101	Accident at the Le Mans trials in 1964, when it was being driven by Jo Schlesser.
102	Accident during tests at Monza in October 1964, when it was being driven by Sir John Whitmore.
110 (X-1)	Group 7 car built by McLaren, revised as a Mk II by Kar Kraft

for 1966. After it had been driven to victory at Sebring it was cannibalized, but the chassis was not destroyed until 1970. A second chassis was built, and this may survive.

111	Reputedly written-off after Bob Bondurant's crash in the 1965 Targa Florio. However, it appears that the damage sustained would hardly have justified scrapping in the normal course of events, and it is reasonable to assume that much of this car was used in later cars (but, whatever its fate, 111 no longer exists).
GT40P/1000	Accident at Sebring in 1966, when it caught fire after Bob McLean crashed into a trackside pole.
1005	Burned in a garage fire.
1029	Accident during practice at Le Mans in 1966 (collision with a Mk II).
Mirage M10001	Accident at the Nürburgring in 1967, when Dr Dick Thompson spun into a Ginetta that had already crashed.

Several other cars have been reported 'scrapped', although it appears that sufficient of some of these survived to become the basis for 'restorations', in some cases amounting to rebuilds from the ground up! Inevitably, the condition of surviving cars varies, and so does their 'original' content. A once carefully-restored car was apparently neglected in Japan

A batch of road cars at FAV in 1966, being prepared for shipping to Shelby-American. These are familiar publicity photographs, and most of the cars were destined to be returned to Europe. A single screen wiper sufficed, but external rear-view mirrors were an essential addition for tolerable rearward vision.

There was a suggestion of the coming 'classic' stature of the GT40 at FordSport Days in the early 1970s, when examples could be bought for a fraction of their subsequent values. This 11-car grid is at Brands Hatch in 1972.

in the second half of the 1990s, a well-known car was wearing its fourth body by that time, another that was finally restored to a condition where it could be entered in an auction was probably best described as a 'bitza', and so on . . .

By the early 1980s, there were more 'GT40s' in existence than had been built at Slough. Some cars were built up from unused chassis and off-the-shelf spare parts – for example, there were six Mk III chassis which were not used in the truncated programme and three of them were later disposed of through P & M Racing Preparations, and JWA sold three directly, while a set of parts also passed through P & M. These chassis were destined to become the basis of GT40s which have been given numbers to follow the Mk III sequence (GT40P 1108-1114) – although two of them are 'ghost' numbers, as they were used in rebuilds of earlier cars, one actually being a replacement chassis used in Bryan Wingfield's rebuild of P1012.

When JWA closed, John Willment retained much of the surviving material. Out of this, a rolling chassis was passed to Brian Angliss to build up as a complete car, which was sold with the chassis number GTP40P 1086 in 1984.

In the second half of the 1990s three more were to be assembled, largely from sets of parts still in original JWA bins stored in a caravan on Willment's Surrey farm. He agreed that these should be built at Bryan Wingfield's workshops, with assembly largely undertaken by Paul Fleming. There was full Ford approval – with some disregard for the JWA period, the company was to claim that this trio completed the early-1960s sanctioned manufacturing run – and the first (1087) appeared on the Ford stand at the 1996 British motor show. The second was to be finished shortly before John Willment died in 1997, with the third to follow a year later.

Some new parts had to be used, notably monocoques (by Tennant Panels, from original factory drawings), suspension members for safety's sake, and of course bag

146

In an enterprising conversion, Jim Toensing created a 'pure' GT40, fitting an ex-Indianapolis quad-cam engine in 1027 to create the car Ford might have built early in the GT40 programme. In the normal-specification car the carburettor was located centrally, whereas in Toensing's conversion this space was occupied by the exhausts, with the primaries bulging slightly above the rear deck line. For this car, the engine was fitted with Lucas fuel injection in place of the Hilborn equipment used in its USAC days. Detuned for road use, it gave around 425bhp.

tanks. The original moulds were used for bodies in the late-1960s style, and durability was ensured with extra layers of fibre matting.

The use of John Dunn's Swindon Engines-prepared 302 CID V8s was appropriate as Falconer and Dunn had undertaken early GT40 engine development; the V8s had Gurney-Weslake heads and four Webers, and the claimed output of 444bhp was verified in bench tests. It also exceeded the output of the late engines installed by JWA by some 20bhp.

As was to be expected, the appearance of the cars is totally authentic, despite tiny departures (for example, the BRM-pattern alloy wheels mount Avon 'historic' pattern tyres).

Apart from those cars built up around genuine but unnumbered tubs, an element of confusion is introduced by the variations in style among the originals, especially as cars in the 'P' series could be finished to individual customers' requirements and a few kits with numbered chassis were sold for completion outside the Slough plant. Beyond that, GT40s completed for circuit use were converted into road cars, and vice versa, while detail modifications could make for surprising changes in appearance – the use of Borrani wire wheels, or cast Halibrand or BRM wheels, or the use of wide wheels on cars such as Paul Hawkins', for example, while some private owners experimented with fins and spoilers, echoing the works team's early aerodynamic struggles (and as far as one can see, to no good end!).

Chassis 1004 provides an example of the confusion that can be encountered. It was built for Shelby American and raced in Rob Walker's colours at Le Mans, returned to Slough and later brought out of store by JW Automotive to be rebuilt as 1084, late in the GT40P series. Meanwhile, parts of its original body had been used in the total rebuild of 1009 after that car had to all intents and purposes been wrecked at Kyalami in 1968. That was so obviously a write-off that its 1968

Bryan Wingfield, founder of the GT40 Owners' Club, a replica builder of distinction and restoration expert, with Mk II 1012, which he reconstructed around the wreckage of the chassis, spares collected from American sources, and some newly fabricated parts – the transmission was made from scratch. This mammoth task was completed in 1983, 16 years after 1012 was 'destroyed' in a test accident at Daytona. The engine bay looks neat and uncluttered, and far from full, although the 7-litre V8 was a bulky unit by mid-1960s standards. A rollcage had been installed in this car shortly before Peter Revson's crash at Daytona, when its value was proved. Wingfield completed P/1000W a little later, in 1984, as a replica GT40, for a high proportion of 1960s components were used with the first complete Tennant chassis. It was numbered to take the place of a car destroyed at Sebring in 1966, with a 'W' added to ensure that it would not be passed off as original. It was widely demonstrated for more than ten years, then 'went out of circulation'.

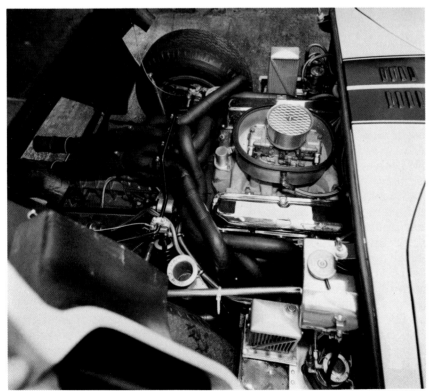

The first of a trio of GT40s (1087) completed in Bryan Wingfield's Essex workshops in the second half of the 1990s. This car appeared on Ford's stand at the 1996 British motor show.

owner, Malcolm Guthrie, commissioned a new lightweight GT40 from Alan Mann, using a spare Mk II chassis, and this car was also numbered 1009, for a while amended to AMGT 1009! However, some time later Bryan Wingfield reconstructed the chassis, and a second GT40P 1009 was built around it . . .

In 1983, incidentally, 1084 reappeared on the circuits, in British historic sportscar races, still to JW Automotive specification and quite properly in the old Gulf colours, the only outward change being a 'Gurney bulge' in the roof as owner-driver Martin Colvill is as tall as Daniel Sexton Gurney.

One Mirage became GT40P 1074 in 1968, and was one of the two late cars in the 'P' series (the other being 1075) which were the mainstay of the Gulf/JWA team. They had lightweight hulls, although any slight gain from this was more than offset by the addition of standard JWA racing equipment – full fire extinguisher systems, heavier radiators, and so on. One of the pair, 1075, had an outstanding career. Built during the winter of 1967-68, it was raced in 1968 and 1969. In 1968 it ran at Daytona (retired), Sebring (retired), Brands Hatch (first), Monza (retired), Nürburgring (third), Spa (first), Watkins Glen (first) and Le Mans (first); in 1969 it ran at Daytona (retired), Sebring (first) and Le Mans (first).

There was little love lost between Slough and the American collaborators when control of the race programme was shifted to the USA, and this is reflected in a detail of the records – when production cars destined to become Mk IIs were shipped out of Slough, the chassis plates were removed (in any case, the chassis plates were flimsy, being attached by two rivets). This introduced a note of uncertainty: eight chassis were laid down at Slough for completion as Mk IIs, but more appeared – 1012 has already been mentioned, and as the value of these cars was belatedly recognized, even the wreckage of 1011, the Mk II in which Hansgen crashed at Le Mans, became the subject of a rebuild, after the Holman & Moody employee who bought the wreck passed it on to an American collector. Incidentally, Mk IIs were to gain Holman & Moody chassis plates, perhaps to mimimize any consequences of liability litigation (the Mk IV plates were to record 'Manufactured by the Ford Motor Company, Dearborn, Mich, USA'). The Holman crew chief from the 1960s thought the cars that were first and second at Le Mans in 1966 had changed identities when one passed through his hands for repair after a race accident in the 1990s . . .

The records show 34 race starts by Mk IIs; 17 retired, and one was disqualified, to give an acceptable finishing record of almost 50% (the four victories fell to Shelby cars, once on loan to Ford France, while Holman & Moody achieved only four finishes).

149

The last J. *Above:* J12 in Brian Angliss' workshops during its restoration – actually, during the first attempt, before it was stripped down and work started again. *Below:* Complete at last, and carrying Rod Leach's 'Nostalgia' badge within its nose number circle. Oddly, its flanks curve to the underside like the earliest J, whereas in the definitive racing Mk IVs the flanks and underbody met at a right-angle. The Cobra gives scale – the Mk IV was not a big car. In the 1990s J12 returned to America, sold to an Arizona enthusiast.

The history of the Js and Mk IVs is much more straightforward. In terms of race achievements the Mk IV programme was extremely costly – the cars recorded only five starts, although they did return two victories and a second place.

There has already been confusion, as the 1967 Le Mans-winning car has often been referred to as J6. Ford repainted this car as a clone of the winning J5 for the New York Auto Show (and later a 'Gurney bulge' was added), before it was given to A J Foyt. In this condition it was later entered in historic events by Peter Lavonas. While he owned it, this car was stripped down at the Henry Ford Museum, where its identity as J6 was confirmed beyond question. J5 has always been at the Museum, where among its identifying details was the crushed floorpan under the driver's seat, which a mechanic with the team in 1967 recalled undertaking to gain valuable extra millimetres of space for tall Dan Gurney!

Two of the Mk IVs were not completed until the 1980s, for cars like this had real 'classic' status as values climbed. There might be some disagreement about these cars, as one chassis was minimal – the last is obviously more desirable, but in years to come it could be difficult to prove J12! One of the two Js that were built for Group 7 racing was wrecked in an accident.

The list which follows details all the original cars, and those in the chassis number sequence that were not completed until the 1990s, but not those that were built unofficially on spare chassis, the Mk Vs, or any replicas. It was originally based on the files of Ford Advanced Vehicles and JW Automotive Engineering, although the Slough plant was not necessarily notified of the first disposal of cars supplied to the Ford Division of the Ford Motor Company. Subsequent changes of ownership through the 1970s have been added – well into the period when these cars were often 'investment classics', and owners were not always enthusiasts – together with some interesting moves in the 1980s. Much of the later information was supplied by Ronnie Spain, and for detailed chassis-by-chassis records there is no better reference than his book *GT40* (Osprey, 1986).

GT40/101　FAV. Crashed (driven by Schlesser) during Le Mans test weekend, 1964.

102　FAV. Crashed (driven by Salvadori) during Le Mans test weekend, 1964. Repaired, to become first GT40 to start in a race (Nürburgring, 1964). Crashed (driven by Whitmore) during tests at Monza, October 1964, and 'written-off'. In the 1970s one of the cars built up on a spare JWA tub acquired a 106 chassis plate.

103　FAV/Shelby American/ W Wonder. Revised to 1965 specification by Shelby, and first GT40 to win a race (Daytona 2,000kms, 1965). Oldest surviving GT40.

104　FAV/Shelby American/Ford Styling/A Turner/J Stringer/P Patton/B Jacobs/ G Lonberger. Revised to 1965 specification by Shelby, third at Daytona.

105　FAV/P Hawkins/J Briggs and H Snow/R Petersen/C Kasper/R Buxbaum/C Kemp/E Dearborn. FAV development car, first to be fitted with 289 engine.

106　Built up by Kar Kraft with 427 CID engine and used extensively in tests in 1965. Cannibalized for parts, but largely survives.

107　Built up by Kar Kraft with 427 CID engine, run at Le Mans as Mk II in 1965 (Amon set lap record in it), then used in test programme.

108　Open car. Shelby American/H Cluxton/J Robertson. Used for automatic transmission tests by Shelby.

109　Open car. Shelby American/ D Jeffries. Ford France entry at Le Mans, 1965.

110　X-1, built by McLaren, with Abbey Panels light-alloy chassis. Later converted to open Mk II, first at Sebring, 1966. Cannibalized and scrapped although possible parts survive in private collection, as does spare chassis.

111　Open car. FAV. Crashed (driven by Bondurant) in 1965 Targa Florio. Returned to FAV, assumed scrapped.

112　Open car. FAV/P Sutcliffe/N Corner/M Sinclair/K Senior. Rebuilt by Peter Sutcliffe as standard coupe, after 1966 Spa race rebuilt as GT40P and converted to refined road car (with improvements such as wind-up windows) by Sinclair.

GT40P 1000　FAV development car, used as mould for body panels of production series. Completed early 1966, loaned to Comstock Racing, destroyed in McLean's fatal accident at Sebring.

1001　FAV/B White (Team Chamaco Collect)/S Taylor/C Lucas/ J Woolfe/A Cox/Malaya Garage/T Smith/S Stevenson/T Mitchell/J Lees. FAV development car, loaned to Essex Wire for Le Mans 1966, converted to road car by Terry Smith in 1970.

1002　F English Ltd/J Macklin/D Prophet/J Pearce/B Classic/R Douglas-Hughes. First GT40 to be raced by private entrant, first to be raced in Britain.

1003　Ford France/T-M Giorgi/R Lamplough/C Young/G Tamplin/ J Broad/R Horne.

1004　Shelby American/JW Automotive – rebuilt to 1968 specification as 1084, then R Clarke/M Colvill. Still energetically raced in Gulf colours, with 'Gurney bulge' in roof.

1005　Shelby American/FAV/T Drury/G Humble/R Darlington/R Vincent/R Fry/Ashmore Brothers/J Seddon/M Hipperson/J Walther (destroyed in fire).

1006　FAV/T Drury/D Leech/T Drury/B Prynn/P Evans/M Basted/M Haywood. FAV development car, first to be fitted with definitive nose. Crashed (driven by Whitmore) during tests at Monza 1965, rebuilt by Terry Drury with Alan Mann body during his first period of ownership. Also crashed when owned by Leech, sustaining nose damage which was repaired by Prynn. Rebuilt to 1965 specification by John Etheridge.

1007   Ford France/P Bardinon/C Duval.

1008   Ford of Britain, first as race-specification press car, then exhibitions car, first as a Mk II 'lookalike' after 1966 Le Mans, converted to resemble 1075 after 1968 Le Mans, exhibited at the Louvre, later fitted with Boss Mustang engine. Restored in 1980s by Bryan Wingfield for promotional services.

1009   P Sutcliffe/E Nelson/M Guthrie/W Skiles/W Cantrell. First GT40 to be supplied in 'kit form'. Wrecked in Kyalami accident in 1968 (driven by Malcolm Guthrie), but rebuilt over two-year period. Meanwhile, Guthrie had commissioned replacement built around a Mk II chassis by Alan Mann and run at Le Mans in 1969. This car later sold to G Jackson. Neither GT40P/1009 was renumbered!

1010   Essex Wire/P Sadler/W Green/T Graham/B Classic/ J Seddon/B Poole. Wrecked in accident during tyre tests at Oulton Park in 1966, rebuilt by Peter Sadler around a new chassis. Later converted for road use.

1011   Shelby American, for completion as Mk II. Apparently destroyed in Hansgen's fatal accident at 1966 Le Mans test weekend, but wreck retained by Holman & Moody and eventually sold for possible restoration.

1012   Shelby American, for completion as Mk II. Holman & Moody/D Davis/ L Digness/W Cantrell/W Skiles/A Harman. Ran at 1966 Le Mans test weekend, loaned to Alan Mann Racing for Spa 1,000kms, badly damaged in test accident at Daytona in 1967 (driven by Peter Revson). Eventually rebuilt in England by Bryan Wingfield around parts of the original chassis, commissioned by Wayne Skiles. Meanwhile, Don Davis had built another '1012' (this passed on to R Wilcox, then R Nagel).

1013   Prototype road car. FAV demonstration car/B Bowles/W Green/P Sadler/E Falzon/London Sports Car Centre/S Smith.

1014   K Richardson/N Corner/M Henry (as road car)/B Classic/V Woodman.

1015   Shelby American, for completion as Mk II. First in 1966 Daytona 24

hours. Holman & Moody/R Reventlow/L Lindley.

1016   Shelby American, for completion as Mk II. Holman & Moody/Harrah's Museum/L Barth. For some time this car was represented as GT40P 1015.

1017   F English Ltd/R Fry/R Vincent/N Moores/Sarnia Ltd.

1018   Shelby American (as show car)/L Murphy/D Piper/L O'Neil.

1019   Alan Mann/P Hawkins/A Fletcher/G Crenier/Hexagon/R Cooper/M Norvik/D Leppia. Roof and doors heightened by Robert Cooper.

1020   Ford Division/Ford France/Le Mans Museum. Revised to 1967 specification, re-presented to resemble 1075 in 1983.

1021   N Cussons/C Crabbe and E Nelson/D Walton (as road car)/Lord Lowson.

1022   N Cuthbert/C Gaspar/L Fernandes/T Bancroft/J Cooper/P Vestey/K Harrie.

1023   Alan Mann/P McNally/M Gartlan/M Charles/J Brierly/B Clouston.

1024   Shelby American/A Whatley/B Bondurant/R Leach/C Stewart/N Hulme/B Angliss.

1025   Shelby American, but completed by FAV (this was one of four cars destined for Shelby that were returned to FAV because of documentation problems). Shell/K Luscombe-Whyte/R Lyons/O Harris/P Sheen (as road car)/Mike Spence Ltd/C Long. Crashed when owned by Long, rebuilt.

1026   Essex Wire/Lord Downe/V Gauntlett/T Goodchild. Crashed at Le Mans 1967, rebuilt through next 10 years.

1027   Ford Division/Metro-Goldwyn-Meyer/C Sechan/J Toensing. Exhibition car, camera car, rebuilt by Jim Toensing with 'Indy' engine.

1028   Road car. Ford Division/D Tallaksen/S Earle/G Schroeder.

1029   W McKelvy (Scuderia Bear). Wrecked in Le Mans practice accident 1966.

1030   Shelby American/FAV/Shell/R Lyons/C Hyams/A Copeland.

1031   Shelby American, for completion as Mk II. Ford France/Holman & Moody. To Japan in mid-1970s (two decades later it was reported to be in sadly neglected state). This car has carried 1047 chassis plate.

1032   Shelby American, for completion as Mk II. Repainted to resemble 1966 Le Mans winner, used as show car, later presented to

Indianapolis Motor Speedway Museum and exhibited at Early Wheels Museum.

1033 Road car. G Filipinetti/O Patino/F Sbarro. Completed by Graber as Geneva motor show exhibit, converted to race specification for ASA ESGA. 'Destroyed' in a fire in 1970, later rebuilt by Sbarro.

1034 J Fielding/P Weldon/G Lassum/G Parlby.

1035 Shelby American/FAV/Shell/Axon Armature Rewinding Co (as road car)/M. Hoskison/Dr M Dawes.

1036 Shelby American/Shell (as road car)/E Bird.

1037 Comstock/Ford of Canada/D Marsh.

1038 Essex Wire/P McNally/J Jordan/J Bailey.

1039 Scuderia Filipinetti/P Bardinon/H Chemin/P Brunet. Converted for road use by Sbarro.

1040 Scuderia Filipinetti/F Sbarro/C Gendroz/H Cluxton/D Silawsky. Crashed Monza, 1967 burnt out (driver Bond). Rebuild started by Sbarro, completed by Charles Gendroz.

1041 J. Blaton ('Beurlys')/F Dauwe.

1042 Brescia Corse/A Coli/Capelletti Mec Auto (badly damaged in fire, slowly restored)/R Castagna.

1043 Road car. Shelby American/R Heeresberger/H Wetanson/L Lindley.

1044 J Moulton/Vintage Car Store/K White/M Graham/A Wareing. Rebuilt by Graham with complete new chassis by GP Metalcraft.

1045 Girling/D Hamilton/D Saunderson.

1046 Shelby American, for completion as Mk II. Le Mans winner, 1966. Used in tests by Holman & Moody, then put into store, when it was generally assumed that it would become a museum exhibit. Ford then had scant regard for its history, but it is extraordinary that such an historic car should be discarded. Rebuilt as road car, then part-restored to Mk II race trim. In 1983 it was shipped to an import/export handling company in Ghent by a New York investor, then sold to G Stauffer.

1047 Shelby American, for completion as Mk II. Run as 'Mercury' at Daytona in 1967. Won 1967 Reims 12 hours. P Bardinon/F Chandon.

1048 Brescia Corse/W Konig/J-P Rouget/J-C Geurie/M Dagorne/J-P van den Dorn. Badly fire-damaged in 1971 Le Mans 3-hour race, restoration started by Sbarro,

completed in Italy in 1990s.

1049 Road car. I G Davis/F Grant III/I G Davis/J Jolly/S Meyer. Delivered with race-tuned engine, etc, and used by Gulf-JWA team, reverted to road specification, race-tuned again while owned by Grant, reconverted to road specification by Davis. T Clark/J Jolly.

1050 Ford Division/General Motors/J Kinsler. Used by GM in development of components such as radiators for mid-engined Corvette projects.

1051 Ford UK/D Benny/B Rattey.

1052 A Allece/U Maglioli/A Coli.

1053 Ford Division/V Damone/D Schulz/R Bretz/B Lundy/D Piper/V Norman/M Wheatley/J Heath/D McErlain.

1054 Ford Division/-

1055 Ford Division/Edsel Ford II/J Mecom Jr.

1056 Ford Division/R Shaw/C Abel/W Hanssen/J Scheberies/H Wetanson/T Powers.

1057 Ford Division/N Nero/V Shields II/N Nero/R Stafford/D Jungerman/R Ash.

1058 Ford Division/A Grillo/H Siegel.

1059 Ford Division/Shelby American/E Schoenherr/H Wetanson/ J Frost. Damaged when stolen from Schoenherr, repaired.

1060 Ford Division/W Arterberry/J Toensing. Damaged by fire when owned by Arterberry, rebuilt by Toensing.

1061 Ford Division/H Heinl/H Vose III/H Wetanson/C Long/B Spicer.

1062 Ford Division/D Brown/H Cluxton/J Lewis.

1063 Ford Division/G Kohs.

1064 Ford Division/-

1065 Ford Division/A Harmon/N Shrigley-Feigl/W Loughran.

1066 Ford Division/A Grillo/H Wetanson/Hexagon/T Harrison.

1067 Ford Division/D Schulz/H Cluxton/G Walther/D Murdoch.

1068 Ford Division/S Johnston/H Heinl/P di Mambro/D Cummings.

1069 Ford UK/A Bamford/K McDonald/T Harrison/W Green/J Robinson/A Hamilton/R Danny/B Ropner/D and K Mather/M Johnson/R Hedge. Damaged by fire when owned by Ropner, rebuild started by Mather, completed by John Etheridge.

1070 Ford Division/R West/W Hill/R Leppla/D Baer/B Gressard. Damaged by fire when owned by Baer, rebuilt by Gressard.

1071 Ford UK/P Weld Forrester/M Finburgh.

1072 Ford UK/J Cussins/B White/W Green/P and M Blankstone/N Edmonds/A Hamilton/F Gallogly.

1073 T Drury/R Fry/D Leech/B Prynn/G Childs/M Johnson/G Stauffer. Crashed (driven by Ron Fry) at Brands Hatch, 1968. Rebuilt around spare chassis by Bryan Prynn, original chassis to K Davis.

1074 Conversion from Mirage M10003, to 1968 specification. Gulf Oil Corp/J Blaton ('Beurlys')/JW Automotive/D Brown/Solar Productions/H Cluxton/A Bamford/S Juda/G Stauffer/H Cluxton. Roof removed by Solar Productions for use as camera car in filming *Le Mans*. Restored (using original roof) by Anthony Bamford.

1075 Gulf Oil Corp, double Le Mans winner retained as exhibit at Gulf head office until 1976, when it was loaned to Indianapolis Museum. Later sold to H Cluxton.

1076 Gulf Oil Corp/D Brown/D Heinl/F Knoop/J Finn/C Kendall.

1077 Yamaha/Y Hyashi.

1078 G Edwards (Strathaven)/A de Cadenet and D Weir/J Etheridge/J Heath/C McLaren/P Rudd. Wrecked in test accident at Silverstone, rebuilt around Mk III chassis by John Etheridge, original chassis scrapped.

1079 J Blaton ('Beurlys')/F Sbarro/Y Caillet. Crashed at Le Mans, 1968 (driver Mairesse). Partly restored by Franco Sbarro, restoration completed by Yvan Caillet.

1080 A Pires/E Marta.

1081 IGFA (later *Deutsche Auto Zeitung*)/S Schneider/H Berger. Converted for road use.

1082 M Martin/S Pozzoli.

1083 Colegio Arte e Instruccao/W Fittipaldi/G Stauffer. Chassis damaged when sills crudely cut open for bag tanks to be removed whilst owned by Fittipaldi.

1084 Rebuild of 1004, q.v.

1085 G Jackson.

1086 Passed to J Willment in 1971 as an incomplete rolling chassis. Completed by Bryan Angliss in 1984, sold through Adrian Hamilton to a US customer as a genuine zero-mileage GT40 – years after the first replica GT40s had appeared!

1087 Built up from parts held by J Willment, with some replacement items, by Bryan Wingfield. Completed in 1986 and exhibited on Ford stand at British motor show before delivery to American buyer.

1088 Built up from parts held by J Willment, with some replacement items, by Bryan Wingfield. Completed in 1997.

1089 Built up from parts held by J Willment by Bryan Wingfield. For completion 1998.

Mk III: 1101 LHD. Ford Division/P Mellon/R Brass.

1102 RHD. Ford UK/Miss P Wyer. Exhibit at National Motor Museum.

1103 RHD. Sir Max Aitken/B Auger/Romans Ltd/R Davidson.

1104 LHD. J Candler.

1105 LHD. H von Karajan/T Brown/R Cooper/M Novik/Dr C Kalko.

1106 LHD. Ford Division/D Morrell/Mrs D Morrell.

1107 RHD. Ford UK as demonstration/show car, after spell in USA with Walter Hayes, now in care of Bryan Wingfield (for Ford).

The cars completed by Alan Mann Racing were not numbered in FAV or JWA sequences, but as follows:

AM1 Alan Mann/Holman & Moody/Shelby American/ Firestone/B Fulp/D Champlin/E Recknagel/L Zane/R Myers. Used by Firestone for tyre tests. Wrecked while owned by Doug Champlin, yet to be rebuilt.

AM2 Alan Mann/P Hawkins/J-M Juncadella (Escuderia Montjuich)/J Pearce/D Farnell/T Roberts/G Stauffer. Paul Hawkins' famous car, revised to Group 4 form (although there have been suggestions that in some respects this revision was no more than needed to satisfy scrutineers).

XGT-1 Built up at Shelby American by Mann's mechanics, revised to Mk II specification. Alan Mann/J Haskell/R Wilcox/Holman & Moody/R Nagel.

XGT-2 Built up at Shelby American by Mann's mechanics, revised to Mk II specification. No record of this car after put in store in 1967.

XGT-3 Built up at Shelby American by Mann's mechanics as team spare. Revised to Mk II specification, served as display car. D Eichstadt/S Wright/D Nichols.

Mirage: M10001 Gulf Oil Corp/M Guthrie/F Williams/A Hutton/P Weldon/H Cluxton/J Schoen/T Clark.

M10002 Gulf Oil Corp. Crashed Nürburgring, 1967. Scrapped.

M10003 Gulf Oil Corp. Converted to GT40P/1074, 1968.

J/Mk IV: J1 Ford Division/R Nagel. At one

154

time this car had allegedly been scrapped during the investigation of Ken Miles' accident, but it survived in original form and was acquired by R Nagel.

J2   Ford Division. Wrecked in Ken Miles' accident at Riverside.

J3   Ford Division/H Heinl/L Lindley. Originally a J, rebuilt as first Mk IV and used with bodywork variations in test programme which proved advantages over Mk II. Harry Heinl acquired it in poor condition in 1970, had it fully restored by Holman & Moody, with elaborate adaptations to equip it for street use in legal, mechanical and trim respects (for example, with a handbrake, radiator fans, stereo and air conditioning!).

J4   Ford Division/Shelby American/D Schutz/H Cluxton/A Bamford/G Stauffer. First Mk IV to be built as such, first to race (winner, Sebring, 1967).

J5   Ford Division/Henry Ford Museum. 1967 Le Mans winner.

J6   Ford Division/A J Foyt/L Lindley/ P Lavonas/J Glickenhaus. A car that has caused much confusion, since it was repainted as clone of 1967 Le Mans winner (it was actually fourth in that race). James Glickenhaus restored it in correct colours, and has covered thousands of miles in it on public roads.

J7   Ford Division/H Heinl/J Schoen/R Nagel. Crashed at Le Mans, 1967, was patched up by Holman & Moody as a show car, full restoration to be completed by Rick Nagel.

J8   Ford Division/Holman & Moody/Harrah's Museum/G Stauffer.

J9   G7A. Ford Division/C Agipou.

J10   G7A. Ford Division/C Agipou. Believed destroyed.

J11/J12   Spare chassis built up by B Angliss at Brooklands in the mid-1980s, for Rod Leach and Colin Crabbe/ George Stauffer/-

Production

Prototypes (GT40 101-112):

Coupes	7
Roadsters	4
X-1	1
	12

Production GT40s (GT40P 1000-1089):

Circuit specification	48
Road specification	35
For completion as Mk II	8
	91

Mk III

Left-hand drive	4
Right-hand drive	3
	7

Alan Mann cars	5
Mirage	3
J/Mk IV	12
	130

Even this modest table misleads, for there are known 'duplicates' (for example, two cars with the chassis number GT40P 1009), and then there are the cars built up on spare chassis sold by JWA, which have been given numbers run on from the Mk III sequence (at one stage a car on one of these acquired chassis plate 102, as it went through a dozen changes of ownership in the 1970s. Safir picked up the sequence for its Mk Vs in the 1980s and 1990s, and two more 'GT40s' crept into that listing (see below).

The Mk Vs

This list of Mk Vs is based on Peter Thorp's records, and completes the production record of GT40s and approved derivatives. The breaks in this sequence are accounted for by the Mk IIIs (see Chapter 12) and 1126 and 1127, which were built around Tennant chassis and some original parts by John Etheridge, and approved by John Willment. There were many variations among the Mk Vs, from the aluminium chassis already mentioned to two cars with bag tanks and original GT40 pedal layouts (1137 and 1138), and 10 cars were supplied without engines. A few cars, notably Jim Rose's 1099, were completed by owners. Some of the Mk Vs were built in the mid-1980s, and recent changes of ownership may be confidential or simply not known.

GT40P 1090	P Thorp/C Heepe/J-P Lafuge. Prototype, with roadster body, completed April 1981.
1091	H Harrfeldt.
1092	L Johnson/J Aiken/R Stewart/F Profera/Japanese owner.

A pair of GT40s taking shape in the busy Shelby assembly shop in California, in 1965, surrounded by Cobras and Mustangs.

1093   G Schultz/C Bultiauw.

1094   A Walker. First car to be fitted with split doors.

1095   B Winer.

1096   D Livingstone/R Stewart/H Dehaven.

1097   K Partridge/K Namiki/C Cox/C Seabrook III. Body and engine fitted in USA.

1098   L Johnson. Semi-race car, completed with race-cam engine with Weslake heads and race tyres.

1099   J Rose. Ultra-light steel chassis.

1100   P Thorp/B Huisman. Roadster with lightweight chassis and carbonfibre body panels.

1115   D Collins/A Lawson/N Spiro/Japanese owner.

1116   C Davis.

1117   D Kirk. Body and engine fitted in USA.

1118   J Robinson.

1119   Lord Max Beaverbrook/P Nichols.

1120   J Willment/\H Charbonneauz/P Olczyk/J Mathews/S Milestone. Third owner installed 6-litre engine.

1121   K Hashimoto. Carbonfibre/Kevlar body panels.

1122   B Williams/M Takada.

1123   D Horgan/E Coomber. Split doors fitted by second owner.

1124   J Sadler. Split doors fitted.

1125   Race Corporation, Hong Kong/B Pack.

1128   D Livingstone/R Stewart/G Becker. Mk II style body panels, split doors; 8.1-litre dry-sump all-aluminium engine.

1129   B Koll/G Rafanelli. Mk II body style, split doors; 8.1-litre engine.

1130   Alan Johnson Racing. Mk II body style, split doors; 8.1-litre engine.

1131   The Fine Car Store/K Namiki. Mk II body style, split doors; 8.1-litre engine.

1132   The Fine Car Store/Prestige Co Ltd, Tokyo/J Pace. Mk II body style, split doors; 8.1-litre engine.

1133   P Thorp. Roadster with aluminium chassis and ultra-light body panels.

1134   R Stewart/T Gibson.

1135   M Schaub. Split doors.

1136   B Wood.

1137   Race Corporation, Hong Kong/B Wood.

1138   H Ganley.

1139   R Stewart. Completed to full race specification.

1140   R Stewart.

1141   MIW Motorenwerk. Full race specification, with wide rear body section.

1142   R Stewart/P Nickinson. Aluminium chassis, ultra-light body panels, split doors.

1143   Y Nakagawa.

1144   E Hubbard. Completed in USA. Split doors.

1145   To be completed in 1998.

14

The Race Record

Win some, lose some

This is a record of the major races contested by the GT40s and derivatives from 1964 until 1970, the last season when the cars were eligible for Championship events. In any case, by this time the GT40 had lost its front-line status – for example, three of them did run in the Daytona 24 Hours in 1970, but while one was placed eighth, it covered only 579 laps, compared with the 724 by the winning Porsche 917, and it was well behind a Corvette and a Ferrari 250LM in the same Group 5. This suggests a car past its prime (as did the only other GT40 placing in the top dozen of a 1970 Championship race, 11th in the 1,000km event at the Osterreichring).

This list covers only international races or supporting events at meetings of some stature, but through the second half of the 1960s, GT40s were raced increasingly in minor events. For example, in 1965, Guy Ligier won several lesser French races, while in 1966-68, Ron Fry won more than 30 minor British races, and in the hands of drivers such as John Jordan, GT40s were still very effective at this level into the early 1970s.

Nowadays, GT40s are popular entries in historic events, while in an odd footnote, one of the modern replicas, the GTD40, was successful in a Swedish GT series for modern cars through the mid-1990s. Unless another type is specified in parenthesis in this list, the cars are GT40s, and some detail of performances in main-line races is given in the main text of the book.

1964
Nürburgring 1,000kms
Hill/McLaren	ret

Le Mans 24 Hours
Hill/McLaren	ret
Ginther/Gregory	ret
Attwood/Schlesser	ret

Reims 12 Hours
Hill/McLaren	ret
Ginther/Gregory	ret
Attwood/Schlesser	ret

Tourist Trophy (Nassau)
Hill	ret

1965
Daytona 2,000kms
Miles/Ruby	1st
Ginther/Bondurant	3rd

Sebring 12 Hours
McLaren/Miles	2nd
Hill/Ginther	ret

Monza 1,000kms
McLaren/Miles	3rd
Amon/Maglioli	ret

Targa Florio
Whitmore/Bondurant	ret

Nürburgring 1,000kms
Amon/Bucknum	8th
Hill/McLaren	ret
Trintignant/Ligier	ret
Attwood/Whitmore	ret

Guards Trophy (Mallory Park)
Attwood	2nd

Le Mans 24 Hours
McLaren/Miles (Mk II)	ret
Hill/Amon (Mk II)	ret

Trintignant/Ligier	ret
Bondurant/Maglioli	ret
Ireland/Whitmore	ret
Muller/Bucknum	ret

Canadian GP (Mosport)
Amon (X-1)	ret

Times **GP (Riverside)**
Amon (X-1)	5th
Scott	11th

Kyalami Nine Hours
Ireland/Sutcliffe	2nd

Governor's Trophy (Nassau)
Amon (X-1)	ret
Scott	ret

Nassau Trophy
Amon (X-1)	ret

Pietermaritzburg Three Hours
Sutcliffe	1st

1966
Daytona 24 Hours

Miles/Ruby (Mk II)	1st
Gurney/Grant (Mk II)	2nd
Hansgen/Donohue (Mk II)	3rd
McLaren/Amon (Mk II)	5th
Sutcliffe/Grossman	9th
Revson/Lowther/Gregory	17th
Ginther/Bucknum (Mk II)	ret
Scott/Thompson	ret
Wonder/Wetanson	ret

Sebring 12 Hours

Miles/Ruby (Mk II Roadster)	1st
Hansgen/Donohue (Mk II)	2nd
Scott/Revson	3rd
Foyt/Bucknum (Mk II)	12th
Holqvist/Jennings	13th
Gurney/Grant (Mk II)	disq
G Hill/Stewart	ret
Whitmore/Gardner	ret
Pabst/Gregory	ret
McLean/Oulette	ret
Ireland/Sutcliffe	ret
Wonder/Caldwell	ret

Scott-Brown Memorial (Snetterton)

Attwood	3rd
Liddell	6th
Bond	7th

Monza 1,000kms

Whitmore/Gregory	2nd
Muller/Mairesse	3rd
Ligier/Greder	6th
Redman/Bond	9th
Scott/Revson	ret
Ireland/Amon	ret

Tourist Trophy (Oulton Park)

Sutcliffe	3rd

Brands Hatch 500

Sutcliffe/Liddell	2nd
Ireland/Amon	ret

Targa Florio

Ligier/Greder	12th

International Trophy Meeting (Silverstone)

Scott	6th
Sutcliffe	ret
Liddell	ret
Bond	ret

Spa 1,000kms

Whitmore/Gardner (Mk II)	2nd
Scott/Revson	3rd
Sutcliffe/Redman	4th
Ireland/Amon	5th
Mairesse/Muller	ret
Hobbs/Neerpasch	ret

Nürburgring 1,000kms

Ligier/Schlesser	5th
Sutcliffe/Taylor	6th
Spence/Bond	12th
Whitmore/Neerpasch	ret
Ireland/Salmon	ret
Scott/Revson	ret

Le Mans 24 Hours

Amon/McLaren (Mk II)	1st
Miles/Hulme (Mk II)	2nd
Bucknum/Hutcherson (Mk II)	3rd
Hawkins/Donohue (Mk II)	ret
Whitmore/Gardner (Mk II)	ret
Gurney/Grant (Mk II)	ret
G Hill/Muir (Mk II)	ret
Andretti/Bianchi (Mk II)	ret
Ireland/Rindt	ret
Ickx/Neerpasch	ret
Ligier/Grossman	ret
Scott/Revson	ret
Sutcliffe/Spoerry	ret

Crystal Palace

Sutcliffe	1st
Liddell	2nd
Redman	3rd

Enna Cup

Casoni	ret

Martini Trophy (Silverstone)

Sutcliffe	6th
Liddell	7th
Bond	8th
Salmon	ret

British Grand Prix Meeting (Brands Hatch)

Liddell	11th

Croft

Liddell	1st
Cussons	3rd

Surfers' Paradise 12 Hours

Sutcliffe/Matich	2nd

British Eagle Trophy (Brands Hatch)

Salmon	2nd
Ireland	4th
Liddell	5th
Rees	ret

Guards Trophy (Brands Hatch)

Sutcliffe	6th

Austrian Grand Prix

Salmon	4th
Casoni	7th
Rindt	9th
Ireland	10th
Spence	ret

Zolder

'Beurlys' (Blaton)	1st

Coupe de Paris (Montlhéry)

Ireland	1st
Giorgi	ret

Dixon Trophy (Silverstone)

Fry	2nd

Paris 1,000kms (Montlhéry)

Attwood/Schlesser	ret
'Beurlys'/Mairesse	ret
Vaccarella/Casoni	ret

Kyalami Nine Hours

Sutcliffe/Love	ret
Hobbs/Spence	ret
Nelson/Crabbe	ret

Cape Three Hours

Hobbs/Hailwood	ret
Nelson/Crabbe	ret

Lorenco Marques Three Hours

Hobbs	2nd
Sutcliffe	3rd
Nelson	5th

Pietermaritzburg Three Hours

Hobbs/Hailwood	1st
Nelson/Crabbe	7th

1967
Daytona 24 Hours

Ickx/Thompson	6th
McLaren/Gurney (Mk II)	7th
Wonder/Caldwell	8th
Foyt/Gurney (Mk II)	ret
Andretti/Ginther (Mk II)	ret
Ruby/Hulme (Mk II)	ret
Donohue/Revson (Mk II)	ret
Bucknum/Gardner (Mk II)	ret
Casoni/Maglioli	ret

***Autosport* Trophy (Snetterton)**

Hawkins	1st
Hulme	2nd
Salmon	3rd
Harris	5th
Nelson	7th
Liddell	ret
Drury	ret
Fry	ret

Wills Trophy (Silverstone)

Hulme	1st
Hawkins	2nd
Salmon	5th
Harris	6th
Crabbe	9th
Nelson	10th

Sebring 12 Hours

McLaren/Andretti (Mk IV)	1st
Foyt/Ruby (Mk II)	2nd
Maglioli/Vaccarella	5th
McNamara/Grossman	8th

Thompson/Lowther — ret
Wonder/Caldwell — ret

Zolder
Dauwe — 2nd

Monza 1,000kms
Schlesser/Ligier — 6th
Piper/Thompson (Mirage) — 9th
Nelson/Liddell — 11th
Ickx/Rees (Mirage) — ret
Greder/Giorgi — ret
Drury/Oliver — ret
Borel/Ballot-Lena — ret

International Trophy Meeting (Silverstone)
Hulme — 2nd
Hawkins — 3rd
Liddell — 4th
Drury — 6th
Harris — ret
Crabbe — ret
Salmon — ret

Spa 1,000kms
Ickx/Thompson (Mirage) — 1st
Sutcliffe/Redman — 6th
Salmon/Oliver — 8th
Piper (Mirage) — ret
Schlesser/Ligier — ret
Nelson/Widdows — ret

Targa Florio
Greder/Giorgi — 5th
Schlesser/Ligier — ret

Martini Trophy (Silverstone)
Hawkins — 1st
Salmon — 2nd
Liddell — 4th
Sutcliffe — 7th
Crabbe — 8th
Nelson — 10th
Gardner — ret
Drury — ret

Nürburgring 1,000kms
Greder/Giorgi — 7th
Crabbe/Pierpoint — 8th
Schlesser/Ligier — 10th
Ickx/Attwood (Mirage) — ret
Nelson/De Klerk — ret

Montlhéry
Dauwe — 4th

Crystal Palace
Hawkins — 1st
Gardner — 4th
Liddell — 5th
Harris — 8th
Sutcliffe — ret
Drury — ret

Le Mans 24 Hours
Gurney/Foyt (Mk IV) — 1st

McLaren/Donohue (Mk IV) — 4th
Andretti/Bianchi (Mk IV) — ret
Hulme/Ruby (Mk IV) — ret
Hawkins/Bucknum (Mk II) — ret
Gardner/McCluskey (Mk II) — ret
Schlesser/Ligier (Mk II) — ret
Ickx/Muir (Mirage) — ret
Piper/Thompson (Mirage) — ret
Casoni/Maglioli — ret
Dumay/Greder — ret
Salmon/Redman — ret

Auvergne Trophy (Clermont-Ferrand)
Hawkins — 1st
Sutcliffe — 2nd
Schlesser — 3rd

Reims 12 Hours
Schlesser/Ligier (Mk II) — 1st
Bond/Sutcliffe — 7th
Pierpoint/Crabbe — 8th
Nelson/Liddell — 12th
Greder/Giorgi — ret
Maglioli/Vaccarella — ret

Wills Trophy (Silverstone)
Liddell — 2nd
Crabbe — 5th
Drury — 6th
Fry — 7th
Hawkins — ret
Lucas — ret
Sutcliffe — ret
Harris — ret

Magny-Cours
Giorgi — 2nd
Schlesser — ret

Mugello
Schlesser/Ligier (Mk II) — 4th
Nelson — 13th

BOAC 500 (Brands Hatch)
Liddell/Gethin — 12th
Drury/Holland — 14th
Sutton/Bond — 16th
Rodriguez/Thompson (Mirage) — ret
Lucas/Pike — ret
Crabbe/Charlton — ret

Enna Cup
Vaccarella — 1st

Karlskoga
Ickx (Mirage) — 1st
Bonnier (Mirage) — 2nd
Crabbe — 7th
Nelson — 8th
Hawkins — ret

Austrian Grand Prix (Zeltweg)
Hawkins — 1st
Vaccarella/Maglioli — 3rd
Nelson — 5th

Neerpasch/Crabbe — ret
Hulme/Lucas — ret

Guards Trophy (Brands Hatch)
Hawkins — 2nd
Liddell — 5th
Sutcliffe — 6th
Prophet — 7th
Lucas — ret

Gold Cup Meeting (Oulton Park)
Hawkins — 1st
Liddell — 5th
Hobbs — ret
Corner — ret
Humble — ret

Skarpnack
Bonnier (Mirage) — 1st
Hawkins (Mirage) — 2nd

Paris 1,000kms (Montlhéry)
Ickx/Redman (Mirage) — 1st
Schlesser/Ligier (Mk II) — 4th
Vaccarella/Maglioli — ret
Giorgi/Jabouille — ret
Corner/Blades — ret

Coupe du Salon (Montlhéry)
Nelson — 5th
Schlesser — ret

Kyalami Nine Hours
Ickx/Redman (Mirage) — 1st
Hailwood/Nelson — 3rd
De Klerk/Prophet — ret

Lorenco Marques Three Hours
Prophet — 2nd
Nelson — 3rd

Pietermaritzburg Three Hours
Nelson/Hailwood — 3rd
Prophet — ret

1968
Daytona 24 Hours
Ickx/Redman — ret
Hawkins/Hobbs — ret
Nelson/Hailwood — ret
Wonder/Cuomo — ret

Sebring 12 Hours
Nelson/Piper — 16th
Ickx/Redman — ret
Hawkins/Hobbs — ret

BOAC 500 (Brands Hatch)
Ickx/Redman — 1st
Hawkins/Hobbs — 4th
Salmon/Piper — 11th
Prophet/Bond — ret
Drury/Holland — ret

Barcelona Six Hours
Muir/Godia — 1st
Sadler/Green — 5th

Spring Cup Meeting (Oulton Park)

Hawkins	2nd
Prophet	4th
Vincent	12th
Humble	ret

Monza 1,000kms

Hawkins/Hobbs	1st
Mairesse/'Beurlys'	7th
Ickx/Redman	ret
Piper/Salmon	ret
Nelson/Epstein	ret
Reaburn/Schenken	ret
Drury/Sanger	ret

Targa Florio

Drury/Sanger	54th

Nürburgring 1,000kms

Ickx/Hawkins	3rd
Hobbs/Redman	6th
Salmon/Piper	14th
Granville-Smith/Raeburn	20th
Sadler/Green	21st
Drury/Sanger	34th
Nelson/Pierpoint	ret
Prophet/Bond	ret

Players Trophy (Silverstone)

Hawkins	3rd
Liddell	ret
Prophet	ret
Fry	ret

Spa 1,000kms

Ickx/Redman	1st
Hawkins/Hobbs	4th
Prophet/Bond	8th
Sadler/Green	9th
Salmon/Piper	ret
Mairesse/'Beurlys'	ret
Drury/Sanger	ret
Humble/Smith	ret
Raeburn/Schenken	ret

Tourist Trophy (Oulton Park)

Hawkins	3rd
Sadler	8th
Prophet/Bond	9th
Liddell	ret

Anderstorp

Hawkins	2nd
Liddell	4th
Sadler	5th
Prophet	7th

Watkins Glen Six Hours

Ickx/Bianchi	1st
Hawkins/Hobbs	2nd
Wonder/Cuomo	15th

Guards Trophy (Mallory Park)

Hawkins	2nd

Liddell	4th
Fry	5th
Lanfranchi	10th
Sadler	13th
Prophet	ret

Nurnberg 200 (Norisring)

Liddell	13th
Hawkins	ret
Nelson	ret
Prophet	ret

Vila Real

Hawkins	3rd
Gaspar	4th
Liddell	7th
Raeburn	10th

Watkins Glen

Ickx/Bianchi	1st
Hawkins/Hobbs	2nd
Wonder/Cuomo	15th

Hockenheim

Hawkins	3rd
Prophet	10th
Raeburn	11th
Nelson	ret
Liddell	ret

Martini 300 (Silverstone)

Hawkins	2nd
Nelson	3rd
Sadler	5th
Prophet	10th
Fry	ret

Karlskoga

Hawkins	3rd
Nelson	5th

Gold Cup Meeting (Oulton Park)

Nelson	4th
Sadler	13th
Charles	19th
Darlington	ret

Zeltweg

Hawkins	3rd
Nelson	ret

Jyllandsring

Sadler	7th

Guards Trophy (Brands Hatch)

Nelson	7th
Sadler	9th
Hawkins	10th
Charles	19th
Fry	ret

Hockenheim

Hawkins	3rd
Nelson	7th

Nürburgring

Hawkins	1st
Nelson	3rd

Le Mans 24 Hours

Rodriguez/Bianchi	1st
Muir/Oliver	ret
Mairesse/'Beurlys'	ret
Hawkins/Hobbs	ret
Salmon/Liddell	ret

Paris 1,000kms (Montlhéry)

Sadler	3rd
'Beurlys'/de Fierlant	8th
Godia/Juncadella	ret

Kyalami Nine Hours

Ickx/Hobbs (Mirage)	1st
Guthrie/Hailwood	ret

Cape Three Hours

Hobbs/Hailwood (Mirage)	2nd

Lorenco Marques Three Hours

Guthrie/Hailwood (Mirage)	1st

Pietermaritzburg Three Hours

Guthrie/Hailwood (Mirage)	2nd

1969

Daytona 24 Hours

Ickx/Oliver	ret
Hobbs/Hailwood	ret

Sebring 12 Hours

Ickx/Oliver	1st
Hobbs/Hailwood	ret
Grant/Ouest	ret

International Trophy Meeting (Silverstone)

Sadler	8th

Wills Embassy Trophy (Thruxton)

Juncadella	7th
Sadler	8th

BOAC 500 (Brands Hatch)

Hobbs/Hailwood	5th
Sadler/Vestey	11th
Kelleners/Joest	16th
Juncadella/Spice	ret

Monza 1,000kms

Kelleners/Joest	4th
Hanrioud/Martin	15th
Sadler/Vestey	ret

Spa 1,000kms

Sadler/Vestey	9th
Kelleners/Joest	10th

Martini International (Silverstone)

Daghorn	10th

Tourist Trophy (Oulton Park)

Daghorn	12th

Nürburgring 1,000kms

Kelleners/Joest	6th

Prix de Paris Meeting (Montlhéry)

Martin	2nd

Le Mans 24 Hours
Ickx/Oliver	1st
Hobbs/Hailwood	3rd
Kelleners/Joest	6th
Gardner/Guthrie	ret
Sadler/Vestey	ret

Nurnberg 200 (Norisring)
Hailwood (Mirage)	ret
Guthrie	ret

Watkins Glen Six Hours
Kelleners/Joest	5th
Grant/Heppenstal	ret

Vila Real Six Hours
Green/Blades	15th
Fernandes/Vilar	ret

Klondike 200 (Edmonton)
Cannon (G7A)	ret

Mid-Ohio
Follmer (G7A)	ret

Elkhart Lake
Follmer (G7A)	ret

Michigan Intl Speedway
Brabham (G7A)	ret

Paris 1,000kms (Montlhéry)
Martin/Piot	5th
Green/Baker	6th
Maublanc/Martin	9th
Juncadella/Spice	ret

Barcelona 12 Hours
Juncadella/Spice	ret
Green/Serra	ret

Hockenheim
Green	8th
Martin	9th

Jarama Six Hours
Juncadella/Spice	3rd

Kyalami Nine Hours
Guthrie/Driver	ret
Hailwood/Gethin (Mirage)	ret

Cape Three Hours
Guthrie/Driver	3rd
Hailwood/Gethin (Mirage)	ret

Fuji Speedway
Cannon (G7A)	2nd

Lorenco Marques Three Hours
Attwood (Mirage)	3rd
Guthrie/Driver	6th

1970

Buenos Aires 1,000kms
Forrester/Martin	ret
Serra/Brea	ret

Daytona 24 Hours
Wonder/Cuomo	8th

Forrester/Hedges	ret
Grant/Marcus	ret

Sebring 12 Hours
Grant/Heppenstall	ret
Forrester/Hedges	ret

Nürburgring 1,000kms
de Cadenet/Forrester	ret

Vila Real Six Hours
Gerard/Green	7th
Fernandes	ret
Weir	ret

Watkins Glen
Cannon (G7A)	ret

Edmonton
Hobbs (G7A)	ret

Elkhart Lake
Cannon (G7A)	ret

Road Atlantic
Yarborough (G7A)	ret

Osterreichring 1,000kms
de Cadenet/Weir	11th

Paris 1,000kms (Montlhéry)
de Cadenet/Weir	7th
Vestey/Gerard	ret

Madrid Six Hours (Jarama)
Gerard/Gaydon	ret

Riverside
Cannon (G7A)	ret

GT40s returned to Le Mans for the 50th anniversary celebrations of the 24-hour race, first run in 1923. This trio is outside the Hotel de France at La Chartre, which was used by John Wyer's Le Mans teams during the FAV and JWA years. Ford France hosted the meeting, with Carroll Shelby the guest of honour at a dinner, and 11 GT40s lapped the Sarthe circuit on the morning of the race.

15

Following the GT40

Replicas and lookalikes

The standing of the GT40 as a latter-day classic is reflected in the number of replicas that have been marketed – more than a dozen constructors have introduced copies, and while some of the short-lived kits, with little more than claims to resemblance, have been pitched at the cheap end of the market, several have been serious efforts. Among these, Safir's Mk V stands out as the only one legally to carry a GT40 designation, and to all intents and purposes is a run-on from the Ford/JWA programme. But others are deserving modern sports coupes . . .

Purists recognize only monocoque replicas and can be dismissive of lookalikes with spaceframes. But some of these have a place in the general motoring scene as well as in an appendix to the GT40 story. In all-round road behaviour and comfort, if not always in measured performance, some of these cars inspired by the GT40 competently match several much-lauded modern supercars, and they give an economical entry into that class of motoring. GT40s they are not... and one day perhaps somebody will research the reported attempts to pass off spaceframe 'GT40s' to gullible would-be owners of a genuine GT40 . . .

Attempts to quote kit numbers invariably mislead, for some kit buyers always give up, perhaps after approaching one of the established constructors for help. The best manufacturers have originated high-quality components such as chassis, while as an example, KVA's bodies have been used by other builders. GT Developments was built up on its GTD40, faltered for a while as it attempted to extend its range to modern supercars, but then found a new momentum – in seven years its production of complete GTD40s and kits reached 400, or four times the Ford/JWA output at Slough.

The first convincing replicas came from Sbarro, in Switzerland. Franco Sbarro has built a wide range of cars since the early 1970s, including one-off show models, luxury and high-performance essays, and replicas of classics as varied as the Bugatti Royale, BMW 328 and Mercedes-Benz SSK. He has also been in the business of restoring GT40s, and the Sbarro replacement tub was in heavier-gauge metal than the original and has been held in some regard by restorers who had experienced the rust problems with Slough-built cars. The first Sbarro GT40 replicas used de Tomaso Pantera elements, and their bodywork proportions were slightly distorted. He then turned to copies that were much closer to the original, and some incorporated GT40 components . . . that could be confusing.

Rarely among replica constructors, ERA Replica Automobiles, of New Britain, Connecticut, were to build monocoques. Its first GT40 copies, run alongside 'Cobras' in the mid-1980s, were assembled KVAs, but from 1986 it built monocoque cars that were very faithful to the original. The tubs were only

Prominent labelling leaves no room for doubt! This ERA replica is in Mk II form.

slightly modified and the other parts were remarkably accurate, albeit the cars were in left-hand-drive form (which meant that the instrument panel looked odd!). In the first cars, the 289 CID V8 drove through a ZF transaxle. ERA offered them in road or race trim and reckoned that a car could be built from a kit for around $30,000 in 1986. Like the Sbarro and Tennant chassis, ERA tubs were an acceptable substitute for the 'real thing'.

Tennant Panels, of Basildon, undertook prototype work for Ford, and were persuaded by GT40 restoration experts to make GT40 chassis components. This led to monocoque rebuilds, and then an agreement to make a batch of tubs (Tennants were responsible for the chassis of the three mid-1990s cars built up by Bryan Wingfield, making them from original drawings and incorporating some old parts).

Tennant components were to be used in the Holman 'GT Mk II' announced in 1990. This designation was acceptable, as among John Holman's papers his son Lee discovered Ford's authority for Holman & Moody to build Mk IIs in the 1960s, and this document was open-ended. Incidentally, Lee Holman had been at Le Mans with the Holman & Moody team in 1967, as a refueller and photographer, and was invited to look after the 1996 re-enactment of the 1966 Le Mans 1-2-3.

His Mk II programme in the 1990s was ambitious, and as the investment was substantial the price tag attached to the car was a deterrent – $600,000 (£400,000). Jim Rose was enrolled in Britain, and Tennant chassis to 7-litre specification were acquired, then further modified, while Rose Engineering built sets of suspension components. The material bought in suggested a run of up to 15 cars, but orders did not follow the completion of the first car.

Some excellent one-off replicas have been built, notably by Bryan Wingfield and Gilbert Mordasini, but really well-made kits on spaceframe chassis can appear as convincing, especially if the right wheels are fitted. The first replicas to appear in numbers were Ken Attwell's KVAs, which stemmed from his dreams of owning a GT40 in the 1960s. The first KVA was a Mk III lookalike – he preferred the lines of its nose, and in any case, as a senior engineer at Ford's Swansea plant he had access to the company's own Mk III (indeed, he had a hand in restoring this car after a filming accident). Naturally, he also obtained Ford's consent to his replica; repaying the compliment, his first blood-red machine was displayed in the reception area of the Swansea plant.

Outwardly, the 1982 KVA 'Mk III' was wholly acceptable, as it was when you followed the 'sit on the sill, swing the legs in and slide down into the seat' drill to enter the cockpit. There, the only immediately obvious change was in the positioning of the speedometer and rev-counter, in order to bring the legally-required instrument in a direct line of the driver's sight, while the latter was angled at the left of the panel.

A KVA 'Mk III' of 1982, nearer the camera, alongside a 1984 'GT40', with 'Gulf' decals in places and of a size not encountered in the JWA days. Pro-trac 50 tyres appear alien in that context, too, but together with Kelly and Goodrich equivalents, were recommended by Ken Attwell as value-for-money high-mileage tyres.

Under the skin, Attwell used a spaceframe – obviously it was more practical for kit construction as well as cheaper. This took all the loadings, so the body panels were not stressed. The 10in wide sills gave protection in a side-impact accident and carried pipes and wires within them (the fuel tank in this car was above the rear axle). Many production components were used, such as the Ford Cortina front suspension and steering rack, the radiator and a VW Variant gearbox. His first car had a turbocharged Ford CVH 1.6-litre engine, the 2-litre Pinto unit or Ford's 2.8-litre V6 being suggested alternatives. The GT40 (or 'Mk I' kit that arrived in 1984, after Attwell had obtained access to an original as a pattern for the nose, would accept the 289 CID 4.7-litre V8 from the outset. The VW gearbox was suggested for use with small engines and either a ZF or an adapted Renault 30 gearbox for larger engines.

Attwell designed his KVA for easy construction and servicing. To this end, the front and rear body sections were hinged on removable pins (the lights were connected by multi-pin jack plugs). The front suspension could be rolled away on its road wheels when four mounting bolts were removed, and an optional subframe was available to mount the engine, transmission and rear suspension. All maintenance could be carried out from above the car.

Attwell's personal car was built from scratch in four months, and it turned out to be the forerunner of many KVA 'Mk IIIs'. By the spring of 1984, 40 kits had been produced, together with six steel frames for GT40

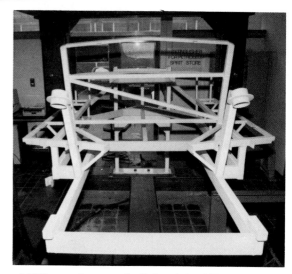

A KVA spaceframe on the Polytechnic of Wales static test rig. Torsional stiffness targets were exceeded, but although this suggested that Attwell could have 'added lightness', he retained his original specification in the interests of impact-resistance.

replicas. One of these was used in torsional strength tests at the Polytechnic of Wales, when targets were exceeded. The 'C' chassis, for 1986, passed the German TuV tests, approved for power outputs of up to 300bhp. This chassis was stiffer and therefore better suited to suspension tuning; it also made for a little more footwell space. Later in the 1980s, carbonfibre/Kevlar was to be offered as an alternative to GRP bodywork.

The first KVA kit cost just under £3,000, leaving the buyer to obtain parts from suspension to power unit – it was estimated that with careful component buying a complete car could be assembled for roughly

GTD pair – a GTD40 (*above*) and a Mk II (*right*), announced in 1991 to coincide with the 25th anniversary of Ford's Mk II victory at Le Mans.

A Mk II engine bay, with the GTD five-speed TX transaxle below the bunch of exhausts.

DAX 40 was a convincing but short-lived clone. Apart from its square-tube spaceframe, bought-in components were used to cut costs, such as Ford Granada or Scorpio hubs with 'Halibrand-pattern' wheels with five-stud mountings (and sometimes dummy spinners to give a centre-lock impression), or Cortina rack-and-pinion steering. Gulf colours inevitably became popular among replica owners . . .

twice the KVA kit price (which was very close to Ford's original projected price for a GT40 in 1965!). By 1990, it would cost more than £20,000 to put a 4.7-litre KVA on the road. Assembled kits had been marketed by Phoenix Automotive, of Goole, in 1984 at prices starting from £14,000, according to specification.

KVA bodies were used by other constructors such as DJ Sportscars, and they made for convincing lookalikes, but Attwell's poor health meant that the impetus went out of the KVA programme in the 1990s.

DJ Sportscars' Dax 40 appeared in 1989, following 'Mk I' lines and being easy to dismiss as a pastiche, especially with the Rover V8 or Renault engines that were suggested. However, it had a square-tube spaceframe in coated steel that had been designed by John Tojeiro and Gary Sanders; it was complemented by Ford suspension

components and brakes. The KVA bodies for these cars were modified in one respect, with the aid of a new mould that resulted in a 'GT40' with an overall height of 42in – the easier access it offered seemed a good idea, but customers wanted a car that was 40in high! In another departure, it was offered in right-hand-drive form, with the gear-lever correctly positioned on the right, or as a left-hand-drive car, with a central shift (there is no record of sales of that version).

In 1991, the rolling chassis and body cost £7,995, but a long list of necessary items from indicator lights to a Ford 302 CID engine (and Holley carburettor) at £2,395 brought the total cost to around £17,000. Approximately 20 Dax 40s were sold before an Indian buyer took over, and the programme ended when he was killed in an aircraft accident. A few of the completed cars had Rover V8 engines, although most had Ford 302 CID units.

Ray Christopher is yet another enthusiast who was seduced by the original GT40, and he attempted to build a replica in the late 1960s. In the next decade he set up Auto International with Graham Kelsey, creating cars for films and TV; they went on to form GT Developments in 1984 and to build the GTD40 to Christopher's design. This has become the most widely known GT40 replica. It was first built at Old Trafford, Manchester, but the company soon moved to Poole, in Dorset, where during the first seven years of the 1990s it produced some 400 GTD40s in either 'modular' or complete car form.

GT Developments did not refer to the word 'kits', with its implication of parts collected from donor cars, but rather to 'modular' cars, which could be bought as partly-built sections ready to be bolted together (for example, the chassis was factory-built to a rolling stage). In 1987, a GTD40 in modular form cost £13,900, but in completed form the price was £26,000 (both figures being less engine and extras – which could be anything from air conditioning to replica Halibrand wheels).

The GTD is built around a zinc metal-sprayed and plastics-coated spaceframe, with a sheet steel floorpan contributing to rigidity. Although in specification terms the suspension follows the original design, the spaceframe means that the usual wishbone rake, giving anti-dive/squat, could not be incorporated, while softer springs are usually fitted, which means that handling is also less taut (although this has not led to any shortcomings in road handling). However, owners tended to fit stiffer springs in place of the normal 200/210 front/rear, accepting the firmer and harsher ride as a price to pay for the reduced roll. Cars built to 'circuit specification' have Rose-jointed suspension, for easy adjustment. Early cars may have had a Ford V6 engine and disc/drum brakes, but the chassis is more than adequate for the 5-litre Ford V8, and disc brakes all round (ventilated at the front) have become the norm.

From the outset, GT Developments had access to original body moulds and have produced their own bodies; normally, these have been in GRP. However, four lightweight cars with aluminium chassis were built with carbonfibre/Kevlar bodies, but Christopher recalls that overall this variant was not a great success, although other lightweights have since been raced.

The usual engine has been the small-block Ford 302 CID V8, rated at 250bhp, and with the tendency to overheat that afflicted cars with this engine mounted at the rear. It drove through a GTD-developed Renault transaxle; the latter does not call for the expertise needed with the ZF box, and it has ratios well

Spaceframe car. In most respects, from dimensions to visual impressions, the GTD40 faithfully follows the GT40 which inspired it. The chassis may offend some GT40 purists, but they can look to the fact that GTD created a fine high-performance coupe with classic lines . . .

167

Taken a quarter of a century apart, these photographs hint at the surprising similarities between the FAV plant at Slough and the GTD factory at Poole. *Above:* GT40s in the 'P' series as production got under way in 1965 (left to right, chassis 1005, 1004, 1003, 1002 and 1001). *Below:* A row of GTD40s at a similar stage in production in 1990, being attended by Terry Bennett, Paul and Mike Christopher, Ken Knight, Pat Murphy, Andy Bennett and Andy McKenzie.

Above: GT40P/1003, destined for Guy Ligier, which was to be campaigned extensively as a Ford France car. Lined up behind it are (left to right) the FAV works manager Pat Murphy, R Hunt and A Deadman, painters Ron Webb and Ron Webb Senior, and D MacPhail. *Below:* A newly-completed GTD40 in 1990. Pat Murphy, by then acting as a consultant to GRD, is again beside the car's left front wheel. Alongside him (left to right) are works manager Simon Osborne, David Free, Terry Bennett, Ken Knight and Trevor Dalton.

matched to the torque characteristics of the engine. The 302 SVO engine gave an additional 35bhp, with more to be gained with components such as the GTD cross-over exhausts.

Almost inevitably, demand from the USA and Japan for a 'big engine' version led to the GTD40 Mk II in 1991. This was given the additional air scoops at the rear, which had made the 1966 cars look so muscular, and was built for the 427 CID Ford V8, rated at 380bhp. The Mk II was to account for around 10 per cent of GTD production.

GT Developments have seen the introduction of other GT40 clones and outlived them into the late 1990s. The company has become a recognized constructor and seen its GTD40s in lightweight form, with dry-sump engines giving over 500bhp, competing successfully in a Swedish modsports series. Like other specialist manufacturers, the company has kept output at a level which means that a few months' orders are usually in hand.

These cars have a dedicated following in the GTD Car Club, which produced a magazine and organizes modest track days, test days and a sprint championship.

Amongst spaceframe GT40 replicas, Ray Mallock's RML GT40 has probably been the closest to the original, and is respected for that. It was launched in 1991, but only a handful have been built – four of them in-house and a fifth – to RML specification – by an outside company in 1997. Three were to road and two to circuit specification.

The RML aluminium-clad steel spaceframe incorporates a roll hoop and the suspension broadly follows original lines, Mallock's considerable experience backing up the computer design. A Ford 302 CID V8 rated at 300bhp was chosen to be standard equipment, as was a ZF 5DS-25/2 gearbox and limited-slip differential (Mallock points out that this meant that the engine could be installed as low as it was in the original GT40). Left-hand drive was feasible, but all the five cars have been built for the British market. A high specification meant a high price – £46,750 when the RML GT40 was announced – but the list of extras, from air conditioning to a racing clutch, was brief. This was a well-thought through, well-engineered and well-equipped replica, conceived in the spirit of the original.

But that can be said of all the other GT40 replicas – or sometimes lookalikes – described in this chapter, for the men behind them have all been inspired by this most classic of performance Fords of the 1960s

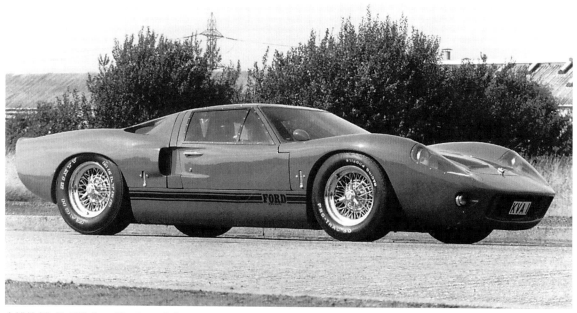

A KVA Mk III. With lines like these, is it any wonder that the GT40 has inspired so many replicas?

16

Specifications

	GT40	MkII	GT40P
Engine			
Cylinders	8 (90° V8)	*idem*	*idem*
Bore	95.5mm/3.72in	107.5mm/4.24in	101.6mm/4.00in
Stroke	72.9mm/2.87in	96.1mm/3.78in	72.9mm/2.87in
Capacity	4,195cc/256cu in	6,997cc/427cu in	4,736cc/289cu in[2]
Valves	Overhead, pushrod and rockers	*idem*	*idem*
Compression ratio	12.5:1	10.5:1	10.0:1[3]
Carburettor(s)	Four twin-choke Weber 48 IDA[1]	Single Holley four-choke 4V	Four twin-choke Weber 48 IDA
Lubrication	Dry sump	Dry sump	Wet sump
Max power	350bhp at 7,200rpm	485bhp at 6,200rpm	340bhp at 6,500rpm
Max torque	approx 275lb.ft at 5,600rpm	approx 475lb.ft at 5,000rpm 5,500rpm[2]	approx 330lb.ft at
Transmission			
Clutch	Borg and Beck 74in three dry plate	Long 10in two dry plate	Borg and Beck 7¼in three dry plate
Gearbox	Colotti four-speed in unit with rear axle (transaxle), no synchromesh	Ford T-44 four-speed in unit with rear axle (transaxle), synchromesh on all gears	ZF 5DS-25 five-speed in unit with rear axle (transaxle), synchromesh on all gears
Chassis			
Chassis/body	0.024in/0.65mm and 0.029in/71mm sheet-steel semi-monocoque with square-tube stiffening and steel roof centre. Glassfibre body panels	*idem*	*idem* except body panels carbon-fibre-reinforced on 1968-69 JWA cars
Front suspension	Independent. Double wishbones, coil springs/shock absorbers and anti-roll bar	*idem*	*idem*
Rear suspension	Independent. Trailing arms, transverse top link and lower wishbone, coil springs/shock absorbers and anti-roll bar	*idem*	*idem*
Steering	Rack and pinion	*idem*	*idem*
Wheels, front	6.00 x 15	8.00 x 15	6.50 x 15
rear	9.00 x 15	9 50 x 15	9.00 x 15[4]
Brakes	Girling disc, 11.5in front and rear	Ford ventilated disc, 11.5in front and rear	Girling disc, 11.5in front and rear[5]
Dimensions			
Wheelbase	95in/241cm	95in/241cm	95in/241cm
Track, front	54in/137cm	57in/145cm	55in/140cm[6]
rear	54in/137cm	56in/142cm	55in/140cm[7]
Overall length	165in/419cm	163in/414cm	168in/427cm
width	70in/178cm	70in/178cm	70in/178cm
height	40.5in/103cm	40.5in/103cm	40.5in/103cm
Fuel capacity	30.5 Imp galls/37 US galls/140 litres	35 Imp galls/42 US galls/159 litres	30.5 Imp galls/37 US galls/140 litres
Weight, dry (all approx) 'start line'	1,835lb/833kg	2,505lb/1,137kg	2,000lb/908kg
(without driver), representative	2,450lb/1,112kg	2,660lb/1,207kg	2,470lb/1,121kg[8]

	Mk III	J	Mk IV
Engine			
Cylinders	8 (90° V8)	*idem*	*idem*
Bore	101.6mm/4.00in	107.5mm/4.28in	*idem*
Stroke	72.9mm/2.87in	96.1mm/3.78in	*idem*
Capacity	4,736ec/289cu in	6,997cc/427cu in	*idem*
Valves	Overhead, pushrod and rockers	*idem*	*idem*
Compression	10.5:1	*idem*	*idem*
Carburettor(s)	Single Holley four-choke 4V	*idem*	Twin Holley four-choke 4V
Lubrication	Dry sump	Dry sump	*idem*
Max power	306bhp at 6,000rpm	485bhp at 6,200rpm	500bhp at 5,000rpm
Max torque	approx 329lb.ft at 4,200rpm	approx 475lb.ft at 5,000rpm	approx 470lb.ft at 5,000rpm
Transmission			
Clutch	Borg and Beck 74in three dry plate	Long 10in two dry plate	*idem*
Gearbox	Colotti four-speed in unit with rear axle (transaxle), no synchromesh	Ford T-44 four-speed in unit with rear axle (transaxle), or Ford torque converter plus two-speed manual gearbox	Ford T-44 four-speed in unit with rear axle (transaxle), synchromesh on all gears
Chassis			
Chassis/body	0.024in/0.65mm and 0.029in/0.71mm sheet-steel semi-monocoque with square-tube stiffening and steel roof centre. Glassfibre body panels	Unit shell of epoxy-bonded honeycomb panels, 0.5in/12.7cm and 1in/25cm thick unstressed glassfibre body panels	*idem*
Front suspension	Independent. Double wishbones, coil springs/shock absorbers and anti-roll bar	*idem*	*idem*
Rear suspension	Independent. Trailing arms, transverse top link and lower wishbone, coil springs/shock absorbers and anti-roll bar	*idem*	*idem*
Steering	Rack and pinion	*idem*	*idem*
Wheels, front	6.00 x 15	8.00 x 15	*idem*
rear	8.00 x 15	12.00 x 15	*idem*
Brakes	Girling disc, 11.5in front, 11.2in rear	Ford ventilated disc, 11.5in front and rear	*idem*
Dimensions			
Wheelbase	95.5in/241cm	95in/241cm	95in/241cm
Track, front	55in/139cm	55.5in/141cm	55in/140cm
rear	53.5in/136cm	55in/140cm	55in/140cm
Overall length	169in/429cm	164in/417cm	173in/439cm
width	70in/178cm	69in/175cm	70.5in/179cm
height	41in/104cm	38.5in/98cm	38.5in/98cm
Fuel capacity	23 Imp galls/27.6 US galls/105 litres	34 Imp galls/41 US galls/155 litres	34 Imp galls/41 US galls/155 litres
Weight, dry (all approx) 'start line'	2,200lb/999kg	1,850lb/840kg	2,205lb/1,001kg
(without driver), representative	n/a	2,290lb/1,040kg	2,650lb/1,203kg

Notes to specifications

[1]Some cars fitted with Holley four-choke. [2] 1968-69 JWA cars: 101mm x 76.2mm/4.00in x 3.00in, 4,942cc/302cu in; max power, approx 412bhp (1968)/425bhp (1969) at 6,000rpm; max torque, approx 396lb.ft at 4,750rpm.[3] 1968-69 JWA cars, 10.6:1. [4] 1968-69 JWA cars, front 10 x 15, rear 14 x 15. [5] 1968-69 JWA cars, Girling ventilated discs, 11.95in front and rear. [6] 1968-69 JWA cars, 57.5in/146cm. [7] 1968-69 JWA cars, 58.5in/148.6cm. [8] 1968 JWA cars, 1969 JWA cars, 2,417lb/1,097kg.

FAV Production GT40P, 1965-66, additional data

Transmission		
Ratios	First 2.42:1	
	Second 1.47:1	
	Third 1.09:1	
	Fourth 0.96: 1	
	Fifth 0.85:1	
	Final drive 4.22:1, 3.33:1 optional	
	Reverse 3.75:1	
Brakes	Girling CR front; Girling BR rear	
Steering	Overall ratio 14:1	
	Turns, lock to lock 2.8	
	Turning circle 37ft	
	Steering wheel diameter 15in	
Tyres	Dunlop, front 5.50 x 15	
	rear 7.25 x 15	
	Goodyear, front 5.50 x 15	
	rear 7.00 x 15	

Fuel system	Goodyear fuel cells; four Autolite Blue Top pumps
Cooling system	Marston light-alloy radiator, 318.75sq in (3in deep); Serck light-alloy oil cooler, 53.2sq in (2in deep)
Electrical system	Alternator, 12-volt, 57 AH
Miscellaneous dimensions	Height to base of windscreen, 28.25in; to top of windscreen, 39.2in; minimum ground clearance, 4in
Weight distribution (oil and water, no fuel)	Front 920lb; rear 1,080lb

Mk V Standard specification (many cars were completed to individual specifications)

Engine	90° V8; 101.6 x 72.9mm; 4,736cc.
	Overhead valves, pushrod and rockers; compression ratio, 9.0:1; carburettors, one Holley or four Webers.
	Max power, 350-375bhp at 6,500rpm. Max torque, 350lb.ft at 5,500rpm.
Transmission	Clutch, AP twin-plate. Gearbox, ZF 5DS25/2 five-speed. Limited-slip differential.
Chassis/body	Sheet steel semi-monocoque with square-tube stiffening. Glassfibre body panels.
Suspension	Independent. Front: double wishbones, coil springs/shock absorbers, anti-roll bar. Rear: trailing arms, transverse top link and lower wishbones, coil springs/shock absorbers, anti-roll bar.
Steering	Rack and pinion.
Wheels	BRM cast magnesium six-spoke. Front, 8 x 15; rear, 10 x 15.
Brakes	AP 12in ventilated discs.
Dimensions	Track, front and rear, 54in/137cm.
	Wheelbase, 95in/241cm.
	Overall length, 158.5in/402.6cm.
	Overall width, 70in/178cm.
	Overall height, 40.5in/103cm.
	Fuel capacity, 24 Imp galls/28.8 US galls/109 litres (twin alloy tanks, with cross-feed).
	Kerb weight, 2,300lb/1,043kg.

(This test report was orginally published in MOTOR RACING magazine, November 1965.)

17

JB TRACK TEST John Blunsden

FORD GT 40

There was a big sigh of relief from our photographer when it was all over. You see, he is a firm believer in the idea that 'things' always happen in threes. The track test of the Ford GT had got off to a bad start when the rear half of the body flew off at about 100mph in front of the pits on the first lap. (There was a good enough reason for this — it hadn't been clipped on! Fortunately, apart from a few grazes and a broken rear screen, it was still in good shape, and was promptly replaced.)

The next incident occurred during a pit stop to change a plug (we had had to start it up from cold on hard plugs, and one of them had objected). Starting up again, there was a very impressive ball of fire from the Webers, and as I simultaneously switched off, floored the throttle and fumbled for the extinguisher, our intrepid cameraman, who had been taking one of his scintillating close-ups of the car's back end, performed an equally impressive backwards-facing standing-start high jump!

After that he was convinced the whole affair was doomed, but when we packed up the only other thing which had become bent (unofficially, of course) was the GT lap record for the short circuit. This was, perhaps, the best compliment that could be paid to this outstanding car, the performance of which puts quite a drain on superlatives.

Let's make it quite plain that this was no fully race-sorted car. It was exactly as it had left the Slough workshops of Ford Advanced Vehicles, since when it had been brought down to Brands Hatch for a few exploratory laps of the short circuit by Sir John Whitmore, then used as a showroom exhibit. John had lapped the car in 56 seconds, and says that with a few 'tweaks', and if he really steeled himself, he could probably get it round in 55 seconds dead. (Current GT record, 57 seconds.) The best I could manage was 56.8 seconds, running the

Goodyears at about 35 psi. Talking to John later, he was of the opinion that the pressures should have been a minimum of 40 psi, and that the difference was probably worth a good half-second. If anyone can name an 'off the shelf' GT car to match these times, first time out, I'd like to hear of it!

The GT 40, as the competition version is designated, comes with a 380bhp at 6,500rpm version of the 289 cubic inch (4,736 cc) Ford V8 engine, running with four Weber 48 IDA carburettors and a compression ratio of 10 to 1. Maximum torque is 330 pounds/feet at 5,500rpm.

SUPERB ZF GEARBOX

Transmission is through a Borg and Beck $7\frac{1}{4}$ inch triple-plate clutch, with quite a light action and a moderate pedal travel, to a superb ZF five-speed all-synchromesh gearbox, with a right-hand shift. There is a sliding lock which makes it impossible to by-pass the second-and-third sector when shifting up from first or down from fourth, plus a flick-down guard protecting reverse position, forward of first. The standard ratios are 2.42, 1.47, 1.09, 0.96 and 0.85 to 1 (3.75 to 1 reverse), with a choice of 4.22 and 3.33 to 1 final-drive ratios. With the lower final drive installed, Brands Hatch became a second, third and fourth circuit, 7,000rpm coming up in third in front of the pits (120 mph), and 6,500rpm in fourth (127mph) being reached at the braking point for Paddock.

The Borrani wire-spoke 15 inch wheels have light alloy rims, and carry 5.50 tyres at the front and 7.00s at the rear, with $11\frac{1}{2}$ inch diameter Girling brake discs immediately inboard of them carrying CR and BR calipers, front and rear, respectively. The rack-and-pinion steering is geared to 2.8 turns, lock to lock, and this feels just about the ideal compromise between responsiveness and lightness.

There is a very robust-looking double-wishbone front suspension system, and the now-conventional rear-end layout incorporating lower wishbones, upper transverse links and parallel radius arms, fully adjustable, of course. The dampers fitted inside the coil springs are also of the adjustable type.

One of the most difficult jobs in driving this car is climbing in or out! It calls for quite a technique — especially climbing out — because the driving seat is well inboard of the outer edge of the body, and the gap between steering wheel and seat cushion, though quite adequate for driving, is a bit marginal for body contortions. If you happen to be tall, you also have to remember to duck your head when closing the door over you, because the roofline is a bare $40\frac{1}{2}$ inches above the ground.

But once you are installed behind the wheel,

the GT 40 approaches the ultimate in racing-car comfort. The ventilated seat, which offers a very reclining driving position, is a fixture, any adjustment necessary being taken up at the pedals. (In fact, things were just about ideal as the car arrived.)

The black decor is most attractive, and the detail finish of a considerably higher standard than might be expected from what is essentially a competition car. The instrument and control layout (white markings on black-faced dials, and matching flick switches, all clearly marked) has been well thought out, and although there are no less than seven dials and 12 switches, you soon learn where to look or feel for the essential ones.

The rev counter, immediately behind the steering wheel, is flanked by the oil pressure gauge on the right, and the water temperature gauge on the left. Then, running further left, we have oil temperature, fuel pressure and ammeter gauges, with, on the extreme left, a large speedometer, angled towards the driver. The switches, lined up below, are in four groups. Running from the left are the sidelights, headlights and pass lights tabs, then come the washers and wiper tabs, and in a third group the dipper and overriding rear light tabs. (This last control is to illuminate a pair of rear lights permanently if the car's normal lights circuit packs up.) The fourth switch group, to the right of the steering column, comprises flashers, left-hand fuel pump, right-hand fuel pump and ignition controls, and there is a separate panel-light switch above, to the right of the oil-pressure gauge.

Two cockpit features became apparent very early on in the test. The first was that it takes a little time to get used to the relatively restricted rear vision — I just didn't see the going of that engine cover! The second was the effectiveness of the cockpit ventilation equipment. In the fairly high ambient temperature of the test, I was very comfortable when travelling fast, but noticed the considerable temperature build-up immediately I slowed down in the pit road.

The next outstanding impression came from the gear shift. Once I had remembered that the shift from second to third calls for a very slight pull to the right, instead of straight back (which lands you in neutral!), it became a dream of a box. It really is a wonderful mechanism, and you can bang that lever around as though you are pre-selecting gears in an automatic transmission. This is a big help coming out of Clearways, because it means that the shift from second to third, which occurs when you've still got quite a bit of sideways 'G' on, calls for the minimum change of torque at the back wheels, and therefore helps to keep the car that much more stable.

HARD WORK FOR BRAKES

The brakes called for quite a firm pedal, and there was quite a lot of squealing from the discs, but presumably this would have died down as the pads became fully bedded in. Travelling at the speeds of which the GT 40 is capable, even on the short circuit, the brakes have to be used quite hard, and once or twice I detected what I thought was either too much, or uneven braking at the back, causing rear-end steering going into Paddock. But on reflection, this was probably the result of too-soft damper settings causing tail lightness over the 'hump' at this point, and upsetting the brake balance. Certainly, after we had screwed up the dampers several clicks all round the trouble virtually disappeared, although I still felt it wise to apply the brakes very progressively at this point.

Being essentially a fast-circuit car, it came as no surprise to find that the GT 40 had been

given a fair measure of built-in understeer, and that if one were to set the car up specifically for the short Brands circuit, rather less understeer would have been chosen. Nevertheless, the only place where it became noticeably time-consuming was up at the hairpin, where about a half-second lift-off just before coming out proved necessary to keep it on a reasonably tight cornering radius.

The comparatively low tyre pressures probably contributed towards a momentary feeling of understeer half-way through Paddock, but this always neutralised itself going into the dip. Otherwise, the car cornered most impressively, and although quite a lot of arm work was necessary to get the best results over the top of Clearways, it was reassuring to find that considerable liberties could be taken with the power to unstick the rear wheels into a very controllable slide. Indeed, standard technique coming out of Clearways seemed to be to provoke a gentle rear-end breakaway and hold the car's attitude on the accelerator rather than by the steering. John Whitmore later suggested to me that with this car we have the best of both worlds — the inherent stability and ease of control of a front-engined design, coupled with the greater competitiveness of a mid-engine layout. This seems to sum it up very well, for though it may not have outstanding 'feel' at the back end, it is most kind to newcomers, and allows them to lap competitively without a long and anxious gestation period — that, surely, is the hallmark of a great design.

This is quite a wide-tracked car (55 inches front and rear, with a 95 inch wheelbase) and there seems to be ample rubber on the road. The ride comfort — probably emphasised by the seat design — deserves the highest praise, and the GT 40 proved completely stable over the notorious rough patch on the apex of the right-hand kink between Kidney and Clearways.

As supplied in the GT 40, the 289 Ford engine is moderately top-endy, with an exhaust note which smoothes out perceptibly above about 4,000 rpm and sounds quite delightful above 6,000. It probably guzzles petrol at an impressive rate from its $30\frac{1}{2}$ gallon fuel cells, but who cares? The cooling system seemed to work well, and despite losing a drop of water through the lack of a sealing ring on the filler cap (someone had 'borrowed' it!) the temperature gauge steadied itself between 75 and 80 degrees F.

I am lucky enough to be offered many interesting and exciting cars for MOTOR RACING track tests, but I can honestly say that not one of them has given me more genuine driving pleasure than this beautiful-looking pale green Ford GT 40. And I'm glad to say that 'things' do *not* always happen in threes!